TAROLOGY

TAROLOGY

Y L

WY EL

/waɪ/ /ɛl/

VOYELLE

ENRIQUE ENRIQUEZ

EyeCorner Press

© ENRIQUE ENRIQUEZ & EyeCorner Press | 2011

TAROLOGY

Published by EYECORNER PRESS,
December 2011
Roskilde

ISBN: 978-87-92633-12-5

Cover design and layout: Camelia Elias

Printed in the US and UK

To Vanessa, w(ho) s(ho)t me twice on t(he) c(he)st and t(he)n s(ho)t me one t(hi)rd time, just like t(ha)t.

T(ho)se w(ho) read my words make t(he)m real. T(ho)se w(ho) don't understand my words make t(he)m precious. For t(ha)t, I t(ha)nk you all.

Contents

TAROLOGY

1. A definition / 9
2. Basic Components / 12
3. Tarology 101 / 15
4. Operation Manual / 17
5. On The Tarologist's Fees / 19
6. My Pledge / 20
7. The Rules of the Game / 21
8. Tarology Tests / 56

READING, TEACHING, LEARNING

1. Reading the Marseille Tarot: The Science of the Circumstantial / 59
2. The Tarot: A Gestural Langvage for the Common Man / 84
3. Seven Ways to Learn Tarot / 85
4. Visual Teaching: The Trumps / 87
5. An Engine Also Known as The Jackalope Theory / 126
6. Tarot's Quarantine / 128
7. How to Turn a Deck of Cards Into a Thermometer / 130
8. Tarot Side-Effects / 131
9. La Conspiration Alphabétique / 132
10. La Conspiration Alphabétique (Appendix) / 134

PATAPHYSICAL POETRY

1. A Pragmatic Paradigm of Pataphysical Paragrammaticism / 137
2. Predicting the Present / 146
3. Letters are Figures of Speech / 150
4. An Infallible Method to Foretell the Time of Imaginary Events / 154
5. A Cutting-Edge Extension to Our Infallible Method to Foretell the Time of Imaginary Events / 160
6. A Case Where Irrefutable Proof of the Pataphysical Nature of the Marseille Tarot is Given, Hoping to Settle the Matter Once and for All / 168

ARGUMENTS

1. A Rather Compelling Allegation in Favor of Using the Marseille Tarot to Predict the Future / 169
2. An Argument On the Benefits Of Looking At The Face Of Beauty And Not At The Rear End Of Knowledge / 175
3. 13 Arguments On The Polisemantic Value Of The Tarot Trumps / 176
4. A little sampler of tarological devices (I) / 178
5. Three Arguments (2+1) On The Concrete Poetics Of The Marseille Tarot (Where One Is Advised To Look At The Finger And Not At The Moon) / 184
6. A little sampler of tarological devices (II) / 186

7. An Argument About Why Le Pandv Is The Only Card That Can Be Reversed / 190
8. A Brief Antinumerological Manual / 191
9. Colormeaning (Moronic Angel) / 198

KEYS

1. A Chapter Where The Marseille Tarot's Key Is Given, While Hinting At The Fact That The Meaning Of An Image Is The Sound We Make When We Describe It, All Done With Such Simplicity That The Formula Itself Is Shorter Than Its Title / 201
2. A Chapter Where The Tarot Is Defined As A 'System Of Deviations', And Also As Something Else / 209
3. Practical Assignments / 214
4. Com(parable) Language / 226
5. Ars Tarotica / 231

TAROLOGY

A DEFINITION

(WARNING: this definition is only valid for the time it takes to read it. Right after that you are on your own).

TAROLOGY: a system of assigning alphabetical value to the tarot trumps*, turning any verbal inquiry into a visual hypothesis, either for edifying or poetic purposes.

The word 'tarology' was coined several years before it had any meaning. Empty, it was left exposed to the elements and was found years later completely filled by salt. It is a tarologist's duty to keep a pinch of this salt under his tongue at all times, as a savory reminder of the fact that pataphysics is the only science that can truly explain the tarot.

Our definition for 'tarology' responds to the sad fact that nothing in our daily use of language will conduce us to spontaneously discover the '*pot a toes*' in the '*potatoes*'. As a vehicle for meaning, language arises from consciousness, while the tarot images conform to a mechanistic unconscious that exists in a state of potential swerve (every card is the *clinamen* of its predecessor) which is independent of any search for meaning unless there is an anomaly in the system. Undisturbed, the tarot is a blind, perpetual motionlessness machine. Human presence is the wrench in that machine's gear, the anomaly that has the card's deviation infused with unexpected significance, usually – and precisely – in ways the conscious mind cannot foresee.

Within this context, the word 'tarology' alludes to the body of practices built around the poetic uses of the tarot as an aleatory device, in the belief that such pursuits can be very illuminating at expanding our repertoire of thoughts about the words we use.

A tarology practitioner is called a **TAROLOGIST**. This term owes its existence to the phonetic similarity between the words 'gist' and 'yeast'. A **tarolo*gist*** is the one who gets the 'gist' of tarology. A **tarolo*yeast*** is the one who, by turning words into images, has his semantic field fermenting. A tarologist creates the conditions for that anomalous moment when chaos makes perfect sense. The *gist* of the *yeast* is to re-create language. Furthermore, the word 'tarologist' is an anagram for *'artist logo'* and also for *'argot toils'*. These notions sustain both the iconic nature of the tarologist's art, and the effort and skills required to master the tarot's visual slang.

Tarology acknowledges two patron saints:

Saint Blaise, healer of obstructed throats, whose name in French means 'to stutter' or 'to lisp'. *'Blaise'* is also a homophone to the English word 'blaze', therefore standing for the thunderous clearing of obstructed language.

Italo Calvino, whose use of the tarot as a generator of combinatorial narratives in his book *The Caste of Crossed Destinies* can be considered an act of plagiarism by anticipation of our efforts.

Tarology is to the occult tarot tradition what the subway's grate was to Marilyn's dress.

* To arrive at the perfect equivalence of 26 cards for 26 letters, all the minor arcana must be eliminated, except for the four aces.

Basic Components

tarology \'la-b(ə-)rə-,tēr-ē-'äv-ēmē-niŋ\

noun
a luminous disruptive electrical discharge of very short duration between two conductors separated by a gas (as air)

intransitive verb
1: suggests a jogging of one's memory by an association or similarity
2: implies a bringing back to mind what is lost or scattered

transitive verb
to ascertain the flavor of by taking a little into the mouth

tarot \'tü-'sē\

noun (the tarot)
1: a semi-illegal mood enhancer
2: oral stimulation
3: a game in which some of the players try to guess a word or phrase from the actions of another player who may not speak
4: a compound that induces altered perceptions of reality, and intense emotional states
5: an organ of copulation

adjective
a form of denying the possibility of defining art

metaphor \'līt\

noun
1: a verbal way to do visually what happens in the body
2: chemical utopia
3: union of genitalia accompanied by rhythmic movements
4: elephant dung

side effects
rash, pruritus (skin inflammation), tremor, dizziness, behavioral changes, agitation, abnormal dreams, drowsiness, excessive sweating, nausea, yawning, painful menstruation, chills

reference
the knife works on the imagination

cognitive dissonance \i-'pi-fə-nē\

noun
1: the sudden obstruction of a blood vessel
2: the part of the action moved by the finger to fire a gun
4: a usually sudden manifestation or perception of the essential nature or meaning of something
5: Joseph Beuys

image \tə-'shāp\

noun
1: neurotransmitter

2: a vessel used for melting and calcining a substance
3: a place in which concentrated forces interact to cause or influence change

form \'laŋ-gwij, -wij\

noun
a process or manner of healing of incised wounds

color \'vo' is\

noun
a substance used to treat something other than disease
a pit flimsily covered or camouflaged and used to capture and hold animals or men

Tarology 101

lesson # 1:
never object to what an image suggests

lesson # 2:
(you are here)

NOTE: print these words right at the center of a page. Read these words over and over with increasing intensity, until you are not there anymore

lesson # 3:
parrot and you will parrot alone
rhyme and the world will agree with you

lesson # 4:
in the tarot, your body is the poem

lesson # 5:
2 of Wands, 2 of Cups
a lion lies down with a lamb
2 of Cups, 2 of Coins
a lamb lies down with a lamb
2 of Coins, 2 of Wands
a lamb lies down with a lion
2 of Wands, 2 of Swords
a lion lies down with a lion
see? it is all about lying

lesson # 6:
it is not so much that one must feel shame of being naked,
but that nakedness has become obsolete

lesson # 7:
carve these words from T.S. Elliot on a soap bar:
"poetry can communicate before it is understood"
wash your mouth with it
spit
now you are ready to hum your readings through a kazoo

lesson # 8:
physical details always merge with abstract notions
if you are looking at a dog, describe it as a cat

lesson # 9:
the image of a hammer
strikes
the person with the force
of what is felt and known
let your words
be a response
to the images,   not
their translation

lesson # 10:
a tumor can be the size of a melon or the size of an orange
it will never be the size of an afternoon
it will never be the size of a rose
you can't have a tumor the size of Rebecca's rage
don't spill your metaphors

Operation Manual

1.
breath through your nose
eat with your mouth
use every hole as nature intended
don't make things something they aren't
tarots are images and they work as such

2.
metaphors are body-oriented
tarots are a set of instructions concealed as body gestures
each gesture has a physiological meaning
each gesture has a metaphorical meaning
shapes are content

3.
each image is a crucible
pouring our thoughts into an image = the image embodies
these thoughts = changing them
an image can enhance our mood
shape is a manifestation of movement
an image suggests a certain behavior

4.
thoughts can be changed by an image
images can change images
changing a definition can change an image
definitions are departure points

5.
meaning shouldn't be a shelter but a trampoline
a cognitive dissonance cracks our egg

6.
the tarot is a laboratory of meaning
to describe = to elicit a 'yes' response = to pace
to suggest = to lead
to answer each question with an enigma = receiver-oriented communication

7.
re-shuffle
repeat

On The Tarologist's Fees

The cost of consulting the tarot varies according to the nature of the questions asked. Since not all questions carry the same weight, it is only logical to adduce that no standard fee can be applied to answer all of them.

As a general rule, an unimaginative question will be charged twice the price of an imaginative one.

Answering any questions dealing with practical matters will be more expensive than answering questions about impractical matters.

Any puerile pursuit will be punished by a high fee. Such fee will decrease proportionately to the percentage of marvel implicit in the question to the extent that an absolutely wonderful question will be answered for free.

In the unforeseen event that a question is exceptionally wondrous to the extent of inspiring in the tarologist a renewed faith in humankind, the tarologist will be the one paying the client the standard fee upon the delivery of his answer.

My Pledge

I will stick chewing gum on your right shoe
I will erase everything but what is red
I will tell you: *"the word 'money' is a dildo:*
Say it until the neighbors feel jealous
pay for the smell of a new car with moans
own the imprint of your toes on your leather sandals"
Do you need a job? Sit on my chair
Do you want love? Sleep with me
Are you ill? Take my kidney
Well, not really
The man behind the curtain went to lunch
I am filling in for him
I am what is left of me
Grab the other end of that wishbone!
I will scream a flower in your mouth:
"Don't be vertical butter! Melt!
Scrap the marmalade off your mind!
Be your thoughts's landlord!
Greet your doubts with an eviction notice!"
The blink before the swoosh smells like lipstick
No one will see the sweat inside your skull
Keep me at eyelid distance
I will become sexist and racist, just like you
I will draw you a future with my tongue on the dust of a window glass
I will write the word "sugar" on my finger and swirl it in your tea to make it sweet

The Rules of the Game

Rule #1

In a world where the notion of art has been expanded outside its traditional boundaries, the tarot becomes a manual for turning life into a poetic mode of being.

Fig. 1:

LL BATELEVR or Le Batelevr or le bateleur

le bateleur

le bas te leurre

the lowest things lure you

le batelevr

le ba   r = le bar = the bar

ba le = 'balè' = balai = broom

ballet = ballet

le bateleur

ba = bas = the bottom of things

or something low

= stockings

le ba l = le bal = the prom

ba l = balle = ball

le bateleur

leur = l'heure = the hour

= leurre = a lure

atele r = atteler = to harness

le batelevr

lev = leV = lever = to rise (with 'le' as in (a tale) and 'V' said as 'v(ain)'+ 'e' in 'padre')

levr = l'è'vr = lèvre = a lip (with 'lè' as in 'let' + 'v' as in 'vain' and a 'r' as if you were roaring!)

levR = le verre = the glass

elev = 'élèv' = élève = a student

= éleV = élever = to raise

vR = vert = the color green

(aller) vers = (to go) 'to' (somewhere)

(un) vers = a rhyme

(un) ver = a worm

vaire = la pantoufle de vair = Cinderella's glass (in fact 'vair') slipper

le batelevr

ba　v = bave = sliver

baV = baver = drool

I like the Tarot of Jean Noblet because it is written 'LL' BATELEVR.

If I say that there are 'two Ls' – in French 'deux L'

I hear that there are 'deux ailes' – 'two wings' !!!

Rule #2

The meaning of something is asking ourselves what it means.

Fig. 2:

If I keep repeating "le fol",

(le fol, le fol, le fol…),

I can finally hear:

"l'oeuf vole"

"the egg is flying"

Faster,

(l'oeuf vole, l'oeuf vole...),

I hear "le vol"

"the flight" or "the theft" (other meaning),

Even faster,

(le vol, le vol, le vol...),

"Vole!" and also "vole-le"

"Fly!" and also "steal it!"

Slowly, the syllabes reverse:

(le...fol...le...fol...le..."folle"),

"a crazy woman".

Le Fol

LeF – Fol

L'oeuf – Folle

The egg - the crazy woman

I focus on French but I realize I am led to a special place if I read "le fol" from right to left:

"lof fel" and say it again and again:

"lof fel, lof fel, lofel, lofel, lofel...(faster)...lofel, lof, lof, lof...

I finally find...LOVE!

another shortcut:

le fol

fol

lof...lof, lof, lof...LOVE again (but faster)

Less fast I get: lof, lof, loflofloflo...

"flot(s)"

"the stream" (and the waves)

Le Fol

L ol: Laugh Out Loud: just have fun!

"Folle" is an anagram of "le fol"

"lof" is a marin term meaning – inter alia – the side of the ship hit by the wind.

You can order "lof" to the helmsman to get the ship to the wind.

In a figurative way, "revenir du lof" (to come back from the lof) means "to moderate anger and claims".

Fascinating: wordplays and puns link to each other:
"lof" refers to "flot(s)"!

You already know about "Le Fov":

We can hear "Le Fauve" – The wild cat (blue animal on the card?)

I easily see the anagram "foule" (the crowd)

If I say "foule", you hear "full … and Fool!"

Le Fov is written with a "v" and not with a "u"

With a "v", we find: fauve (which can also be a color: tawny), and also Lov(e)!

With a "u", we have: le fou (the madman), foule (the crowd)

I could add "foulé" – "trodden"

Fig. 3:

I like the Tarot of Jean Noblet because the Trump n°13 is named: **"lamort"** (Death)

"La Mort" contains: lame (or l'âme)+or

blade (or the soul)+gold

If I read aloud all the letters I read and hear "La MorT" – La Morte (the dead woman)

Also: "la mort la"... gives fast: "mort la" or "mords-la!" (bite her!)

Read in reverse "trom al" sounds like (as said in a common language nowadays faster and faster; elliptical and using apocopes)

"trop mal" as in "j'ai trop mal" ou "ça fait trop mal"

"I suffer too much" or "it hurts too much" – body or mind meanings

Personaly, I would say "trop mal!" in a sarcastic way to express I am not in pain or that what I feel (which is supposed to be physically or morally painful) is just nothing!

I see in "la mort":

la ort - "l'aorte" – "the aorta" ... a letter makes the difference!

(The aorta being a vector of life!)

la rt – "l'art" – "art"

Rule #3

Any text is a potential field for investigating language's own unconscious.

Fig. 4:

Lemperatrise or imperatris or L'Impératrice

imperatris

imper = (un nombre) impair = an odd number

(commettre un) impair = committing a blunder

(un) imper = a jacket

rat = (un) rat = (a) rat!

lemperatrise

lemp rise = l'emprise = hold, ascendancy

pr i = prix = price

(un) prix = (an) award

pr   i e = pri'é' = prier = pray

e p r   is(e) = épris(e) = enamored

e p   a r s = 'é'pars = épars = scattered

em   is = 'é'mis = émis(e) = issued

ra r e = rare = rare

In his book *Le Pèlerinage des Bateleurs,* Jean-Claude Flornoy explains that "L'Impératrice" is the model of the mother.

The young child gets from her the teachings of 'Administer' and 'Circulate' (money, family, household).

That's why I choose to extract from her and not from another one this fragile, particular and invaluable verb:

'Aimer' – 'To Love':

In "L'Imperatrice" is nested:

m er   = M+er = Aimer = 'To Love'

m er   = (la) mer = (the) sea – (the) ocean

m er   e = m'è're = mère = Mother... Mother+Sea+Love=

'Mother is an Ocean of Love' !

Fig. 5:

"**lemperevr**" said slowly, we find phonetically:

lem (l'an)= the year

(lent)= slow

lemp (lampe)= a lamp

per (peur)= the fear

eur (heurt)= a clash

(heure)= hour

I also hear and find playing with the letters:

lemperevr ... empLeVr = ampleur (with "v" pronounced as "u"): which means "magnitude"

pLerer= pleurer and pleureur

to cry and weeper

We also have an internal anagram:

'emperler': beaded (garnished with pearls)

Finally, in "lemperevr" we have

lemp+ereur

lampe+erreur

lamp+mistake

In a correct French "père" (lem-pere-vr) needs an "è"!

– pere – I can read and hear (saying two mute "e") "peu-reux" - "fearful"

– per – or "perds!" and "(il) perd"

"lose!" and "he loses"

I can also read (taking care of the "v")

lem-pe-reV =

r'è'+v = rêve (a dream)

Fig. 6:

lemperance

lemp = lampe = lamp and so as found in 'lemperevr'...

erance = errance = wandering

rance = rancid

l   ance = lance = a spear

anse = anses = handles (she is holding!)

temperance

tem = temps = time

temps = weather

temp = tempe = temple (from the head)

temper　e = temp'é'r'é' = tempérer = temper

emper　= emp'è'r = ampère = ampere

empe　= hampe = shaft, stem

ta　n e = tan'é' = tanner = to tan, to badger

ta　nce = tanc'é' = tancer = to scold

Rule #4

Letters are carriers of movement. Individual letters are highly compressed scores intended to produce a behavioral response.

Fig. 7:

Le Pape

If I keep repeating "Pape": pap(e)pap(e)pap(e)...I fast get papapapapapa...Papa!

Daddy!

I put the "e" into () because in French the final "e" in "pape" is mute.

But if I pronounce the final "e", I get:

papepapepapepapepa...pepa:

"peux pas!" (literally: you may not (do this or touch that), as a daddy would say to his little child)

le pape

l ape: la paix (peace)

laper (to lap)

le pa: le pas (the step)

le+pa=pa+le=pâle (pale)

le pape...if you shake the letters a little you get

'appele' - appeler - to call

and

'epel' - épelle - spell!

If I turn the two 'p' around, I get two 'b' and

If I shake a little the letters I get

'babele' – 'babeler' – a Belgian French expression which means 'to chat'!

[and the (tower of) Babel?]

Fig. 8:

le diable

bL = belle = pretty

aB = abbot

a le = aller = go

(un) aller = one-way ticket

allée = path, Avenue

le D bil = a moron

D bil = feebel

In French 'un' diable is a common name given to a transport trolley.

'Le Diable' has got an anagram
deblai = d'é'bl'è' = déblai (rubble, excavation slope)

Fig. 9:

La Papesse

La Pa: l'appât (the bait)

apese: apaiser (appease)

pese: peser (to weigh)

pes: pèze (slang for 'money' or 'dough')

La   sse: lasse (tired)

l'as (the ace)

L   esse: (une) laisse (a leash)

laisser (to let, to leave)

Pa sse: passé (the past)

passer (to proceed)

La Pances:

You already know (la panse) could mean the "belly".

In French 'panse' is used for animals or to mock (kindly or nastily) people who drink and eat too much (beer belly).

In typography the round part of a letter (as in b, d, or p) is a 'panse'.

'Panse' contains

'anse' (cove)

'an e' - âne : a donkey (or a jackass)

I had already searched the meaning of "pances" when I got the Dodal and the most interesting thing I could find was in "le dictionnaire de la langue françoise" (ancienne et moderne, volume 1 et 2) de Pierre Richelet:

"Pance: a foundry worker's term. Pances: the place where the clapper hits the bell."

'pance': contains three homophones if pronounced 'pancé' (with the same short and dry "say")

penser – to think

pensée – a thought

panser - to dress (healing meaning)
to groom

Rule #5

For the letter, life started on the air.

Fig. 10:

LA MOVREV or LAMOVREVX or L'Amoureux

LA MO R = La Mort = Death

A VRE = (un) havre = (a) haven

LA V E = laver = to wash

REV = (un) rêve = (a) dream

REV = rêver = to dream

OVR = (les) ovaire(s) = ovaries

LAMOVREVX

LA X = l'axe = axis

LA V EU = l'aveu = the confession

V EU = voeu = vow

V EUX = voeux = greetings, whishes

L'Amoureux

mou = (qqch ou qqun de) mou = (sthg or so) flaccid or flabby

mou e = moue = pout

L e x = lex = lex (Dura lex, sed lex)

re x = rex = (latin) = Roi (King)

Fig. 11:

lechariot

lecha = le chat (the cat)

lechar = le char (the tank)

(a) 'chariot' (in English) means (un) char (in French)

le chariot

le   ri = le riz (rice)

Rio de Janeiro!

r ot = (un) rot (a burp)

r oT = roter (to belch)

hari+c+ot = haricot (bean)

le ch iot = le chiot (the puppy)

l(è) ch R

(or) chair = the flesh

chair : homophone 'chèr' = expensive

"   'cher – chère' = dear

HA = (un) achat = (a) purchase

chari T = charité = charity

le c a o = le chaos = chaos

le c ar o = le carreau = the pane

carreau (square -playing cards)

Fig. 12:

IVSTICE or "justice"

jus : juice

just e: juste: just, fair

 V   ICE = vice = vice

V   I E = vie = life

S C = essai = test, trial, essay

(Justice is "severe" and doesn't give many things).

Rule #6

All written words are rendered from the perspective of the reader. We rarely look at words from the letter's point of view.

Fig. 13:

lermite

ler:

l'air (the air)

le (phonetically : lè)

laid: ugly

lait: milk

...mi: do, ré, mi! (or C,D,E!)

mite:

mite: moth and its homophone:

mythe: myth

mité: moth-eaten

Repeated rapidly, I find another character in "lermite":

lermitelermiteler...(slow down)...

Mmmmmmmmm?.........Hitler?!

Hitler:

hit-ler

hit-l'air (to hit the air)

hit=frapper

frapper l'air...or "avoir l'air – frappé –"

"to seem – lunatic–"

I want to substitute an element by another one:

"ler-mite"

l'air (the air) + mite

la terre (the soil, humus) + mite

terre+mite=termite! (a white ant!)

Shortcut:

In modern French, we must write: l'ermite

If I forget the definite article "L" and focus on the name "er-mite", I fast get : ermi...termite: termite (the white ant)

Could I add:

lermite

er ite

(or even more simple)

r-i-t (prononce the letters in French and separately)

èrité = hérité = inherited

I find :

rite: a rite

Rule #7

The tongue speaks lead, the ear hears gold.

Fig. 14:

LA ROVE DE EORTVNE or LA ROVE DE FORTVN or La Roue de Fortune

La Roue de Fortune

Fortun = fortin = un fortin = (a small) fort

For un = forain = les forains = stallholders or fairground entertainers

(adjectival form = fairground)

Phonetically we hear in 'fortune' = fort+tune = (un) fort+(les) thunes

(a) fort+ dough

fort(e) = strong

Roue = rouer (de coups) = thrash

roue = euro = Euro

La Rove de Eortvne

'rove+de' = dévore(r) = devour

d Eor = dehors = outside

dehors! = out!

E t e = été = Summer

Fig. 15:

FORCE

contains:

FOR: fort (strong)

(un) fort (a fort)

(le) for (intérieur): inwardly

FO: faux (wrong, fake)

(une) faux – a scythe

FO C : (le) foc: jib

FO+C = fossé = ditch

+homophone 'faussé' (fausser): 'distort(ed)'

FORC: pronounce F+OR+C: forced

forceforcefor... gives "effort" and "s'efforcer"

"effort" and "to strive"

OR E: orée: edge

FOR E: forer: to drill

OR = GOLD

ORC: un orc (orque): an Orc, a humanoïd creature (in old English, a kind of demon)

CRO: croc: fang

F+R(air)+O+C = féroce = fierce

FROC: frock

Fig. 16:

"le pendv" or "le pandv":

I fast find reapeating "le pendu"..."le pendu le"..."le pendule"

"the clock; a pendulum"

"le pandu":

– pan – (de vie, de mur): a slice of life, a section of wall

Or pan! ... bang!

Un paon – a peacock

– pan – read as "panne": a breakdown

"le pendu":

– pen – I hear "peine": sorrow

Rule #8

Tongues are bridges.

Fig. 17:

'la maison diev' or 'la maison dieu'

you already know the:

l'âme et son dieu = the soul and its god

and the homophones:

l'âme and lame (soul and blade)

'la maison diev'

la m son = l'hameçon

the fishhook

son = sound + homophone

son = bran

mai = Mai = May

mais = mais = but

mals = maïs = corn

'diev' is an anagram of 'vide' (empty)

So we get:

la maison vide = the empty house

I can also find:

la maison dieu with 'diev' written with a 'u' (modern French)

but even phonetically, gives:

diev

dieu = d'yeux (of eyes)

so:

la maison d'yeux = the house of eyes

I relate this meaning to Trump 20, for example.

The 'trumpet-angel' is holding a flag = un drapeau

which phonetically gives exactly: drap+peau = sheet (bed)+skin

I understand it as a sheet made of skin (as the house made with eyes)

(drapeau contains

apeau = appeau = decoy)

'diev' can give:

'devi' = de vie = of life

so:

la maison diev

la maison de vie = a kind of retirement house for (mentally) disabled persons.

In Egypt, 'la maison de vie' was a particular place of the Temple; a library and a training center for scribes and priests.

It's also a term used by freemasons for their initiatory groups.

Phonetically:

l'âme est son(s) de vie = the soul is sound(s) of life

l'âme et son devis = the soul and its quotation

la ma = lama = Lama or llama

la maison diev

a m N = Amen!

a m n e = amener = to bring

maiS = messe = Mass

on di = on-dit(s) = hearsay(s)

Rule #9

Only consonants* are real.

Fig. 18:

"Lestoille" or "le toille":

I can read and hear "les toiles" – "the paintings"

Other meaning of "toiles": "les toiles d'araignées" – "the spider's web"

If I reapeat "lestoille, lestoille, lestoille"… I can hear "lestoil-let" – "the toilet"!

and the homophone "les toilettes" – "outfits"

"le toille"

I hear "le toi" – "le toit"

"the roof"

Also found if I read "lestoille" as "les (lait, laid) toi(les)"

"the (milk, ugly) you – roof (webs and paintings)

"lest" contains "l'Est" – "East"

(du) "lest" – "ballast"

And another homophone "leste" – "nimble"

If I read "lestoille" in reverse I hear a surname and a cooking ingredient:

"elliote sel": "Eliot"+"sel" - "Eliot"+"salt"

selle(s): saddle (faeces)

Fig. 19:

La lvne (written with a "v", said as with a "u")

I hear

"l'alu" = "aluminum"

I find:

la lune

a une: "aune": a kind of tree (alder)

a unit of measure (ell)

The expression "à l'aune de" means: "by the yardstick of"

la lvne:

la v e: lave – lava

(je) lave – (I) wash

or lavé orlaver: washed or to wash

If I take care about the "V" I find:

la lvne

Vne – phonetically:

Véne: veine: vein or its homphone

(de la) veine: luck!

Finally, I find someone I didn't expect in "La Lune":

la lvne

a lun: "alun" – "alum": a salt used as astringent, emetic,... (in deodorant for example)

In French, "alun" is pronounced the same as "ALAIN" ! So, I can say that 'I' (Alain) am in the Moon (La Lune)! ('Je' (Alain) suis dans 'La Lune!'). In English, the right expression is: "to have one's head in the clouds".

Fig. 20:

Le Soleil

Le sol (the ground), phonetically:

le sot (the idiot)

le saut (the jump) and its homophone:

le seau (the bucket) and its homophone:

le sceau (the seal)

le soleil

l o eil = l'oeil (the eye)

"lès oleille": "les oreilles" - ears!

*Consonants are made of teeth, tongue and lips.

Rule #10

An absence of meaning would be the ultimate luxury.

Fig. 21:

LEIVGEMENT or (in modern French) – Le Jugement:

An easy one!

Phonetically, (and even orthographically), we easy get:

Le Jugement

Le Juge ment: The Judge is lying

(The one who judges lies)

ju   ment: (une) jument: (an) ass

Ment: (un) aimant: a magnet

aimant: (somebody) loving

geme: (une) gemme: (a) gem

LEIVGEMENT:

I.V.G. = I(nterruption) V(olontaire) de G(rossesse)

= Abortion

V e ment = V+é+ment = véhément = vehement

L VGE = (une) luge = (a) luge

Fig. 22:

LEMONDE Le Monde

(we already mentioned the anagram):

Le Monde : Le Démon (The Demon)

Le Monde

L'   onde: L'ond : The wave

Le Mon   : Le Mont: Mount

Le   de : Le Dé: The Dice

Le   de: L'è'+de: Laide: Ugly

Mo de: (La) Mode = Fashion

Mon: Mine

noM: Le Nom: (The) Name

+ homophone:

non: Non!: No!

'Le Monde'

Le Mo nde = Le Mot 'NDE' ... = The Word 'NDE' (a well-known acronym: Near Death Experience)

'NDE' said in French gives phonetically "Haine Des 'E' " – "The Hatred of (the letters) 'E' " .

I wanted to know what happens when an eclipse occurs; what's happening when the 'typographic incarnations' of the sun and the moon meet each other?
Let's see!

le soleil

la lune .... If 'la lune' hides 'le soleil', we have to hide the letters they have in common: (as a soustraction)

(-) _____

(=) e a s o i l u n are the letters left.

Let's shake!

e u n o i a + s l

Do you see what is left after a solar eclipse......................" eunoia" !!!

You know the moon can't hide the sun totally. Here, 's and l' remain.

's' + 'l' = sel = salt

There's always 'un grain de sel' (a pinch of salt.)

An eclipse gives a salted 'eunoia'.

s

eunoia

l

NOTE: all the 'illustrations' for the rules of the game are courtesy of Alain Jacobs.

Tarology Tests

1st tarology test *(to be uttered with a deep breath)*

test \'an(t)-sər\

noun
1: a cognitive engine
2: a rhetorical question
3: a paradox to be meditated upon that is used to abandon ultimate dependence on reason and to force sudden intuitive enlightenment.

Please qualify the following statement:

La Papesse is La Maison Diev right before Force opens the lion's mouth

( ) true

( ) false

( ) March 19, 1314

( ) all of the above

2nd tarology test *(the difference between information and experience)*

test \ri- 't'or-i-kəl\

noun
1: an inspirational catchphrase
2: a puzzle consisting of small pictures that are to be fitted together to form a sentence
3: a wad of indigestible material (as of bones) regurgitated by a bird of prey

Please qualify the following statement:

If the skeleton takes ~~te~~ Bateleur's hand I can have my Ace of Batons

( ) René Lavand

( ) true

( ) rannoch moor

( ) false

3rd tarology test

test \kəm-ˈper\

noun
1: a conjuring trick requiring manual dexterity
2: correspondence in function between anatomical parts of similar structure and origin

Please qualify the following statement:

~~What~~ Ivstice does and the charioteer doesn't: separate the master from the idiot

( ) the right hand doesn't know what the left hand is doing

( ) false

( ) ignore green

( ) true

4th tarology test

test \ə-'na-lə-jē\

noun
1: a two-images retrospective of Matthew Barney
2: a group of cartoons in narrative sequence

Please qualify the following statement:

~~L~~estoille and ~~T~~emperance: the cremaster muscle
( ) marina abramovic – rhythm 10 (the star, 1999)

( ) true

( ) so true

( ) so very true

READING, TEACHING, LEARNING

Reading the Marseille Tarot: The Science of the Circumstantial

On the Pataphysics of the Marseilles Tarot

1.

Olde time meat   the Ace de Batons

All the time meat   in Lempereur's hand

All the time eat   is like Le Pendu's pole

2.

Poet André Bretón, who always championed the Marseilles tarot, also championed the writings of Jean-Pierre Brisset. Brisset's whole body of work was devoted to show how man descended from frogs. Beyond the memorable claim itself, what makes Brisset's work fascinating is that all of his evidence was...

linguistic! Take this sentence from Brisset's *The Science of God, or The Creation of Man*, published in 1900:

> *J'ai un l'eau, je mans* (I have the water, I ea(t)), *which became j'ai un logement* (I have a home), *shows us that the first home was in water and that people ate there.*

In his writings, Brisset would see the formal connection between the (French) words used to name two seemingly unrelated domains – men and… well, frogs – as objective proof of their scientific connection. It is no wonder that he is considered a pataphysics's saint! His linguistic escapades are of interest here because his wordplay is very close to what the French define as *la langue des oiseaux*, a game mainly based on homophonies, in which the duplicity in the sound – shape – of words would be used to recall duplicitous meanings, but also, unlikely connections which could be either amusing or inspiring. Moreover, Brisset's connection with pataphysics is significant here in that pataphysics might allow us to place the Marseille tarot within the broader context of a poetical tradition, both from a chronological, and an operative point of view.

Pataphysics is defined as "the science of exceptions" (although we may have reasons to believe this was an exception!). It is suggestive to think that the Marseille tradition has always used the tarot within a pataphysical context, even if, or precisely because, it has done so unconsciously. Perhaps it would be more sobering to say that the Marseille tarot's tradition unconsciously belongs to a whole school of French poetry that grew from Alfred Jarry's pataphysics and informed, directly or indirectly, groups like Dada, Surrealism, Oulipo, and many others.

Card-maker Jean-Claude Flornoy suspects there was a visual stage of *la langue des oiseaux* (the language of the birds) that could have predated the verbal one. Contemporary authors working with *la langue des oiseaux,* such as Luc Bige and Yves Monin, focus entirely on the written word. Even so, that kind of wordplay resembles the idea of finding connections between the details in tarot cards that are typical of the Marseille tarot tradition ("card number Thirteen shows Le Fou's skeleton", "the wall behind the twins we see in Le Soleil card conceals the tomb we see in Le Judgement"). The circumstantial connections hinted by these visual homophonies are taken as positive proof of some actual knowledge being hidden in the images by their makers. A direct result from this is the deliciously masturbatory, and rather pataphysical, maxim: "the proof that there must be a secret in there is that we don't know it". This thesis belongs to what we could call the Marseille tarot's 'folklore' – a parcel within its history – which has been fostered by some French authors active in the 20th Century – the 'pataphysician's century – such as Tchalay Unger, or Philippe Camoin.

The Marseille tarot's folklore is made from little circumstantial connections, like "Justice carries around her neck the rope to hang Le Pendu". (This is a rather an exceptional claim, since no rope can be seen around Justice's neck in any other tarot, and even in the Marseille tarot it can be said we are looking at a robe's lace). Since these coincidences don't amount to a whole, cohesive, system or design, they fit very well into a "science of exceptions". Even so, all these arbitrary visual connections are taken as tangible proof of the card-maker's intention. While the reading of these details as a rather crippled body of hidden knowledge offers no advantage to our objective understanding of the Marseille tarot's history or iconography (unless we understand folklore as a slice of history), it represents a whole quarry for pataphysical poetry. It is said that "Actual works within the pataphysical tradition tend to focus on the processes of their creation, and elements of chance or arbitrary choices are frequently key in those processes". Just as the members of the Oulipo group were notorious for imposing capricious restrains on their work, whoever reads the tarot accepts to create a meaningful narrative while being subdued by randomness and mathematical probability. (In the benefit of the circumstantial, it should be noticed here that Italo Calvino was at some point considered an Oulipo member. His *Castle of Crossed Destinies* was composed under very specific constraints implicit in using all the cards of a tarot deck, spread on a table, in one single arrangement.)

Given that the poetics of the tarot are the poetics of Chance, and given that Calvino's process (like any non-moralizing reading of the tarot) can be seen as more memorable than its final result, we would like to submit *The Castle of Crossed Destinies* to the hall of fame of pataphysical literature. Then, we would like to challenge Alejandro Jodorowsky's definition of the Marseille tarot as a "metaphysical machine" by re-defining it, instead, as a "pataphysical machine"; for, the tarot cannot be used to understand what is real, but to understand how what isn't real can become realizable. In his book *Pataphysics, the Poetics of an Imaginary Science,* poet Christian Bök, writes: "For pataphysics, any science sufficiently retarded in progress must seem magical". By turning whomever uses it into a pataphysician, the Marseille tarot becomes a tool of unmatched obsolescence to face the future. If

Alfred Jarry, the father of pataphysics, defined it as "the science of imaginary solutions", we can confidently use his definition to account for the process of choosing a life's course based on a random selection of tarot cards!

3.

Ace de Deniers: filigreed = I feel greed

4.

Up until now we* have struggled to conciliate the verifiable findings of tarot history with the poetics of the Marseille tarot. Iconography tells us that the tarot trump cycle presents quite a specific message: "Only Virtue trumps over the vicissitudes of Life". Although this powerful message brings forward the brilliance of the trump cycle's design and allows for a sober homiletic usage of the tarot, it also limits the possibilities of reading anything else in the cards. The message allows for no exceptions! At odds with this message we have the French optical tradition, which suggests that the Marseille tarot responds to a holographic scheme in which a 'secret' has been hidden in the interrelationship of the smallest details we see in the cards. We celebrate this thesis as an unconscious poetic gesture. (The pataphysic nature of this claim is also unconscious. These authors don't see anything subversive in proposing the absence of unicorn food in a pet shop as positive proof of unicorns being elusive creatures).

Still, the problem remains. An adherence to the tarot's iconographic message reduces the analogical games that are possible to play with the cards. The solution to this conundrum is given to us by the concept of **anagram**. If we take the trump cycle in its original order as our 'source' sentence, we understand that by anagramming that sentence, or sections of it, we obtain several new anagrams of that source sentence, and each one of these new sentences reveals new messages and meanings. We believe this to be a very important notion.

Along with homophony and etymology, anagramming and reversing words are viable ways to discover what they conceal. The same devices can be applied to the Marseille tarot. After all, those are the fundamental gestures in *la langue des oiseaux*. We submit that the importance of these word games for the Marseille tarot tradition has been unjustly overlooked. The French play with the details in the cards in the same way they play with the sounds of words! The Marseille tarot tradition is a by-product of the unique relationship the French have with their own language. This is an extraordinary finding. As outsiders, we can only marvel at the unfathomable fact that most French tarot authors prefer to take this connection for granted, while favoring more arcane pursuits. Not only does the French language lend itself beautifully to homophonies, but the French love to play with them.

While analyzing Brisset's oeuvre (*Sept Propos sur le Septième ange*, Paris 1970), Michel Foucault offered a fabulous metaphor: "the chances of a die falling on the same side seven times in a row are unlikely". But Brisset has shown us that the same word could mean seven different things! The implications of conceiving each one of the Marseille tarot's images as a dice that won't necessarily fall on the same number every single time we lay it on the table are extraordinary. This allows us to turn every reading of an image into its own exception. (It also allows us to say, "*Foucault made me do it!*")

For the Phoenicians, the letter X marked a spot. Water holes are a vital fixture in maps, and the letter X shows a fox's head drinking water on a pond, its face reflected on the surface of the water. A fox will only come for a drink if it is safe. For the Phoenicians, the letter O represented an eye and the letter K represented the lines on the palm of a hand. 'O.K.' shows an eye looking at an empty hand, confirming that there is nothing concealed in it – no weapon to kill foxes – and therefore all these foxes – whose names have the letter X right on the middle – know that it is O.K. to come where the X marks the spot, and drink. Since it is safe, all kinds of animals will come too from the four corners of the earth to quench their thirst, just as the letter X suggests. (X is the Roman numeral for 10.

Now we know why, in the tarot, the numbered cards show the higher number of elements). Our insistence on using the alphabet to illustrate our understanding of the Marseille tarot hopes to underline both the fact that the Marseille tarot functions exactly like a language does, and that the way we use language mirrors the way we think. Words are naked thoughts. When images take the place of words, they become naked thoughts too. The French's proclivity for pattern recognition accounts both for *la langue des oiseaux* and for The Marseille tarot optical language. They are both the visual and phonetic halves of the same poetic coin. In *The Castle of Crossed Destinies* Calvino tells us that the *As de Deniers* (ace of coins) is a coin that someone flipped but ended up standing entangled in some bushes: neither tails nor head! That is a pataphysical coin toss.

There is one word in French that contains all five vowels: *oiseaux* (bird). For the English language that word is *eunoia* (beautiful thinking). There is more than one of such words in Spanish, most notably *eufonía* (beautiful sound) and *eulogía* (beautiful speech). Interestingly, if we take vowels to be the soul of a word, we will see how *eunoia, eufonía,* and *eulogía* all share the same soul! We cannot help but find magic in the way all these five-vowel words allude to elevated things.

The French language allows for an exceptional playfulness that has turned the Marseille tarot tradition into a unique house of mirrors.

The Marseille tarot tradition has transformed the exceptions of its own language into a system. To taste the pataphysic nature of this kind of poetry, two delicious examples should suffice. The first one comes from Philippe Camoin. (Camoin's method to interpret the Marseille tarot takes us immediately to a pataphysic world, starting with the fact that, although he acknowledges that the Marseille tarot brings within itself the keys to its own decoding, he claims to own these keys). Camoin gives us the Law of Two, which states that "Two cards often share a relationship"; except when the Law of Three is at play, in which case "Icons may come in Threes, the third version may show a variance"; except of course when the Law of Four is at play, in which case "Icons may come in Fours, the fourth version may show a variance". Camoin even has a Law of Exception! This one basically reverts his Law of Resemblance, in which "Numerous examples abound wherein cards have iconographic resemblance to each other". That is, the cards always resemble each other, except when they don't.

Our second example comes from Tchalai Unger. As if the title of her book: *The Tarot, an Answer From The Future* (Paris 1985), weren't pataphysical enough, here we have a little pearl that would have made Brisset very proud:

> To call 'the fool' the card that bears the name 'Le Mat' is to deprive ourselves from a very rich source of information, (count the more common letters in all the tarot's names, which words do they create?). Besides, it would be like freezing the card's meaning while suppressing all the weight the unconscious gives to homophonic games. Indeed, the name doesn't just operate at the level of mere spelling, but also in a phonetic sense. The Mat, from the Arabic mat – death – is only used in chess in reference to the king, who cannot leave its place without being captured. Besides, the mat – who has no number nor place – is outside of the tangible order, and even so, he is leaving. This apparent paradox gets enriched by other additional meanings. Matte is a mixture of copper and sulphur; an object lacking luster, from the Latin mattus, the mast from a ship, which is perpendicular to the bridge and allows the sails to propel the boat forward.

In both Camoin's and Unger's cases, reality is just a departure point from where we are soon removed through successive jumps. While each leap's length seems reasonably short, the overall effect is consistent with what writer Pablo López has defined as 'pataphor', this is, "an extended metaphor that creates its own context" or even better: "that which occurs when a lizard's tail has grown so long that it breaks off and grows a new lizard."

Therefore, we can describe the Marseille tarot tradition as a true 'science of the circumstances', where iconographically irrelevant details acquire a fundamental importance and everything we see is taken to be part of a bigger, albeit non verifiable, scheme. Here we are, once again, before Brisset's gesture of making a universal theory out of untranslatable connections among words. Such consistent inconsistencies leave us with a wealth of pataphysical poetry to delve into. It may be difficult to accept that the Marseille tarot didn't need the conscious gesture of its makers for the French to find in its images the same rejoice they found in language. But let's not go there. Perhaps it would be better to believe that Noblet, Dodal, Conver et all, all early card-makers, were also pataphysicians.

5.

la maison dieu

l'âme et son dieu

6.

We suggest that the Marseille tarot divinatory tradition belongs to a broader French literary tradition, represented by a lineage of writers who, inspired by the puns and wordplay that were part of French popular culture, used *la langue des oiseaux* as part of their creative methods. (Interestingly, Richard Khaitzine's book *La Langue des Oiseaux, Quand ésotérisme et littérature se rencontrent,* proposes *la langue des oiseaux* as the underlying link between the work of Raymond Roussel, Alfred Jarry, Maurice Leblanc and Gaston Leroux).

Who belongs to that lineage? It would be impossible to determine where it all began, but we can signal a few signposts, starting with François Rabelais, who left us an intriguing invitation in the prologue to his Gargantua and Pantagruel:

> In the perusal of this treatise you shall find another kind of taste, and a doctrine of a more profound and abstruse consideration, which will disclose unto you the most glorious sacraments and dreadful mysteries, as well in what concerns your religion, as matters of the public state, and life economical.

Many authors have been puzzled and inspired by these lines, most notably Claude-Sosthène Grasset d'Orcet (1828-1900), who outlined a whole methodology to find the hidden "taste" of Rabelais's work, using what in his own words was *la langue des oiseaux*. It is important to notice how Grasset d'Orcet thought that not only literary works, but also images, should be decoded by using *la langue des oiseaux*.

Grasset d'Orcet's method consisted mainly on scanning the text and choosing words with homophonic potential, so their sound can suggest a different arrangement, a new sentence, that will have him discovering a new meaning within the text. (He allegedly used a grid, and took care of rearranging these words to form eight-syllabe sentences, preferably ending in L, or in a L-sound). For example, from the sentence: *"Et fut trouvée par Iean Audeau, en un pré qu'il avoit près l'arceau gualeau..."*, Grasset d'Orcet would choose the words *"iean Audeau-pré-arceau gualeau"* whose sound, together, would be taken to mean: *"Janus, dieu pairé arche Gaule"*. Notice how poor Jean Audeu ended up becoming God Janus *(Janus, dieu)*! This may be hard to see in print. (This seems to be one of the reasons why this is called *la langue des oiseaux* (language of the birds), as it only exists while the sound of a word is 'flying' to where it remains ambiguous, jumping from one semantic field into another one. This all stops when the sound is 'caged' in print).

The key for Grasset d'Orcet's operation lies in the notion of homophony. In a rather simplified example, if we were to read aloud the name *'Loraine'* in French we will notice how it sounds like *'L'or reine'*. We could then say that, in *la langue des oiseaux*, Loraine means "gold reigns". If we are on a roll, we could even say that we have found the *Reyne de Deniers*'s first name.

In the tarot, the folklore has it that when we pronounce *La maison dieu (The house – of – God)* in French it sounds like *l'âme et son dieu (The Soul and its God)*. When we pronounce *Le bateleur*, it sounds like *le bas te leurré (That what is low lures you)*. As soon as we recognize the way these homophonies expand the original meaning of these cards, we experience the operativity of *la langue des oiseaux*. (Consistently with a "science of exceptions", there are only a handful of card names that lend themselves to this game).

If the eight-syllabe scheme was used, and the L rhymes were respected, we would arrive at what Grasset d'Orcet called *grimoire blanc*. When the procedure included referencing words from foreign languages, such as Latin or Hebrew, he would call *grimoire noire*. If both the eight-syllabe and the L-rhyme schemes weren't followed, Grasset d'Orcet would call it *Lanternois*. (We must keep in mind that *Lanternois* is one of the language spoken by some characters in Gargantua and Pantagruel).

In his book, *Petit dictionnaire en langue des oiseaux,* Luc Bigé describes Lanternois as "reading a text without the vowels". This seems as a useful simplification within the same methodology of letting the sound of words dictate the combination of new sentences. By extracting the 'soul' of words we are left with their bodies, and these bodies can be 're-animated' by giving them a new 'soul'. That 'soul transplant' is precisely what Grasset d'Orcet achieved: same carcass, new meaning. All these methods seem to bring forward both the 'physicality' of words and the immateriality of speech. A conjunct of letters becomes like a flute which, when we blow air through it, achieves a certain sound. Different pronunciations are different ways of 'playing' these word-instruments to elicit different associations, or emotional responses. If, for example, we take out the vowels in the word SOUL, we are left with S L. Giving that 'body' a new 'soul' (by exchanging the original vowels with two different ones which will occupy their exact same place) will leave us with words such as SEAL or SAIL or SOIL. Now, it is just a matter of finding how the words 'seal', 'sail', and 'soil' expand our understanding of the word 'soul' to have a pataphysic ball.

Grasset d'Orcet also used a device that would be of special interest to us. He called it *Patelinage*, that is, expressing the text with gestures instead of words, as in a game of charades. *Patelinage* seems to mean *'playing the fool'*, and it comes from *'Patelin'* who seemed to have been a popular character, of cunning manners, in some theatrical farces. In a game of charades, we hope that the literal description of a gesture would make representational, metaphorical, sense. Something similar happens here. A proposed reading of an image through *patelinage* would consist on describing the figure's posture, gestures, or details, and then detect potential homophonies for the words we use to describe these attributes.

If we were to look at *L'Ermite*, for example, we could take the fact that he is holding a lantern as a wink to Grasset d'Orcet, as if *L'Ermite* were saying with his gesture *"Look! I can show you lanternois!"* If we were to look at the *blaze* on top of *La maison dieu*, while remembering that the French term *blaise* (From the Latin *Blaesius*), means *'to lisp'* or *'to stutter'*, and that Saint Blaise was famous for healing obstructed throats, we could be inclined to think that *La maison dieu* is saying *"Clear the throat! Stop stuttering!"*. (The pataphysical nature of these gestures should be evident, as they all suppose by using an initial degree of separation from reality as a trampoline to achieve further degrees of separation).

One author seemed to have taken Grasset d'Orcet's advice to the letter: Fulcanelli. In his book *Le mystère des cathedrales* (1926), we find this enchanting assertion:

> For me, Gothic art (art gothique) is simply a corruption of the word *argotique* (chant, slang), which sounds exactly the same. This is in conformity with the phonetic law, which governs the traditional cabala in every language and does not pay any attention to spelling. The cathedral is a work of art goth (Gothic art) or of argot, cant or slang. Moreover, dictionaries define argot as 'a language peculiar to all individuals who wish to communicate their thoughts without being understood by outsiders'. Thus it is certainly a spoken cabala. The *argotiers*, those who use this language, are the hermetic descendants of the argonauts, who manned the ship Argo.

(We have to point out, tough, that the argonauts preferred to plug their ears with beeswax rather than listening to the mermaid's chants).

There was another French wordsmith, Gerard de Nerval (1808-1855), who is thought to have said:"Heraldic is the key to understanding the history of France". Perhaps Nerval was answering to Victor Hugo, who said that coats of arms were: "the symbolic hieroglyphs of feudalism". We take these comments as demonstrative of a sensibility towards symbols that may have been the basis for French occultism, and which manifests itself beautifully in French literature. Following the pataphysic example of our predecesors, we have found a link between Nerval and the tarot: Gerard de Nerval was known for keeping a lobster as a pet, under the argument that lobsters were peaceful and would never bark nor sniff one's manhood. (We were almost sold to that last argument until we noticed how the French word for lobster is *homard* whose anagram, *'Ah, Mord!* literally means *'Ah, Bites!*) The lobster's name was Thibault, and Nerval liked to walk it on a leash around the Palais Royal in Paris. Now we know why there are two dogs and a lobster in *La Lune*. It is obvious that the image-makers who conceived that card committed an act of plagiarism by anticipation, at least three centuries before Nerval was born!

Besides Fulcanelli, it was Raymond Roussel (1877-1933) the author who provided self-professed proof of this connection between *la langue des oiseaux* and French literature. Roussel explained his method (*Comment j'ai écrit certains de mes livres*, 1935), which he called his procédé, like this:

I chose two similar words. For example billiards and pilliards. Then I added to them words that are similar but taken in two different directions, and I obtained two almost identical sentences. Having found the two sentences, it was a question of writing a tale which can start with the first and finish with the second.

Again, homophony turns certain words into doors between separate semantic fields. In Roussel's hands, *les lettres du blanc sur les bandes du vieux billard* (the white letters on the cushions of the old billiard table) became *les lettres du blanc sur les bandes du vieux pillard* (The white man's letters on the hordes of the old plunderer). Due to the *procédé*, words become living organisms, whose cells split and propagate by a series of homophonies, associations, and puns. Sounds familiar?

Roussel was a poet's poet, revered by his peers but never fully appreciated by the public at large. Michel Foucault has devoted many pages to Roussel (*Death and the Labyrinth: The World of Raymond Roussel*, 1986). He is not alone,of course. From André Bretón to John Ashbery, many poets have acknowledged the tremendous impact Roussel had in their work.

André Breton intuited a connection between Roussel's antics and alchemy. Foucault downplayed the connection. Ashbery reasonably argues that we may never know. So far, nothing suggests that such link is fundamental to fully appreciate and apply *la langue des oiseaux*. As a matter of fact, what writers have done with *la langue des oiseaux* for pure literary purposes seems to exceed what the occultists have achieved with it. The reason soon becomes aparent: the methodology outlined by both Grasset d'Orcet and Roussel suggests that *la langue des oiseaux* is a game that doesn't *reveal*, but *creates* meaning. This language doesn't have us finding metaphysical truths, but founding pataphysical realities. Perhaps that is the 'taste' Rabelais wanted us to palate: the taste of language itself, inviting us "to extract wealth from it's own poverty", as Foucault would put it. Nothing in the methodology itself suggests someone left a message hidden in those texts in the first place. When we take a text and recombine its parts until a new text emerges, we aren't uncovering an occult message, but creating new meanings that weren't necessarily implicit in the original text. As with any exercise in pattern recognition, we are very likely to find whatever we are looking for, unless we aren't looking for anything, in which case we may just enjoy the surprises that words conceal. If what we find uncovers new aspects of the original texts – if we find out that the bite is implicit in the lobster – we are primed by our brains to adjudicate such coincidences to the will of an 'agency'. We would submit that 'agency' is the distance that separates the occultist from the poet. Where the poet sees the beauty of words brought forward by his own talent, the occultist sees a divine plan.

7.

if a snake's egg grows roots

its tail will sprout an apple

8.

In the Phoenician alphabet N stands, or slithers, for a snake. Perhaps that is why we find it in both GARDEN and EDEN. The snake brought the end of Paradise by making Adam and Eve face themselves in the mirror of their nakedness. The letter N is symmetrical to itself, if we rotate it 180 degrees clockwise or counterclockwise. The letter N is the letter I looking at itself in a reversed mirror, so the reflection of its head is where its feet should be, the reflection of its feet is where its head should be, and both reality and reflection are always ready to switch places.

Le Pendu is a man standing on his head while looking at us as if we were a former, upright, reflection of himself. Looking at *Le Pendu,* we become the letter N.

As a game, the main peril *la langue de oiseaux* could bring us is madness.

In his *Homo Ludens* (1938), Johan Huizinga defined play as "a voluntary activity which takes place within certain fixed limits of time and space, according to rules freely accepted but absolutely binding, having its aim in itself and accompanied by a feeling of tension, joy and the consciousness that it is 'different' from 'ordinary life'". Madness has our compulsions turning us into machines. Its rules are binding but not freely chosen. It has been said that madness is the creative response of an individual to cope with a frustrating environment. Pataphysics, the science of the imaginary solutions, can be seen as a form of self-prescribed madness. While a madman is sequestered from ordinary life, a pataphysician is self-sequestered from reality. We can see how, as a pataphysical machine, the Marseille tarot can help us reach those two degrees of separation with reality that pataphysics prescribes, but a warning is in order: we may end up eating the bread crumbs trail we left behind to orient ourselves, never finding our way back home.

9.

Amusing: *Le Tarot contient de 22 lames ses leçons*

I'm using: *Le Tarot qu'on tient, devin de lames, c'est le son*

10.

Imagine you are standing in front of a brick wall. Initially, all of these bricks look exactly the same. When you think about them, you envision them all serving the same purpose: to build a wall. But after passing your hand over the wall you discover that, here and there, some bricks are loose. If you move the loose bricks a little bit, you take a peek into another world beyond that wall. You cannot quite see that whole world, but these different glimpses allow you to form a picture of it. It doesn't matter if the picture is accurate or not. What is important is that these loose bricks have taken you beyond the wall.

With their methods, both Grasset d'Orcet and Roussel evidenced language's loose bricks. While Grasset d'Orcet's gesture resembles the passing of the hand over the wall to sense the loose bricks left by the builders, Roussel built a whole city whose walls had loose bricks in them. As Roussel points out in his *Comment j'ai écrit certains de mes livres*, the procedure was akin to rhyming: one has to go around tapping on each brick to find the hollow ones.

Perhaps, a typical reading of the Marseille tarot based on *la langue des oiseaux* seems closer to Grasset d'Orcet's than to Roussel's approach. The tableaux conformed by a sequence of cards seems to us like the brick wall which, being already there, is inviting us to find its 'loose bricks'. For example, in a sequence conformed by *Le Toille, Le Monde* and *l'Empereur,* we will immediately notice how each one of these cards shows a bird. We could say that the bird is a 'loose brick' that connects all these three images. Once we have detected it, the pattern created by these three birds moves to the foreground. The rest of the figures become 'solid bricks', useful only to give context to the loose ones. Reading the birds as a pattern: when the little black bird (in *Le Toille*) rises (as on *Le Monde*) it becomes a symbol (as in *l'Empereur*), and it will be our message. Perhaps the Marseille tarot's folklore is right, and these birds we see on both *l'Empereur* and *l'Impératrice's* shields are a direct allusion to the canting arms of medieval heraldry. We could then see these three symbols saying: '*the tarot's symbols speak bird*'.

This methodology is fairly consistent with the mechanics of a classical tarot reading: given a random selection of cards we would impose the grid of our personal concerns to it, until some symbols start clicking and we perceive a message. That is Grasset d'Orcet's gesture, a gesture of decoding.

Roussel's gesture, that of the poet, would imply building a sequence of cards based on the 'loose bricks' we find in them. Let's say we start with *l'Empereur*. Now we go through the whole deck, looking for a card containing a piece of *l'Empereur*. (Such gesture isn't short on insights. After all, we are defined by the choices we make). Choosing *l'Impératrice* to accompany *l'Empereur* based on the symmetry among birds would present us with a whole different range of narrative possibilities than if we would choose *Le Pandu* to accompany *l'Empereur* based on the fact that both have their legs crossed. More important, this initial gesture would define two completely different sequences of cards.

We have now a beginning in *l'Empereur* and an ending in *Le Pandu*. If we, loosely, follow Roussel's procedure, what remains is a matter of going through the whole deck again until we find one card that could link the previous two. If after *l'Empereur* we have chosen *Le Pandu*, we could notice how both *l'Empereur* and *Le Pandu* have a bent knee. The French word for 'knee' is *'genou'*, whose anagram is 'Ego nu', this is, 'naked Ego'. This would make either *Le Toille* or *Le Monde* our most likely choices. (In *Le Monde* we see both *l'Empereur's* bird and *Le Pandu's* crossed leg). Let say we chose *l'Impératrice* to accompany *l'Empereur*. Which card can bridge them? The French word for 'bird' is *'oiseaux'*, which is anagram for *'eaux soi'*, this is, 'water oneself' and for *'aux soie'* which means *'with silk'*. *'Eaux soi'* could take us to *Le Toille*, who is bathing in a river; and *'aux soie'* takes us back to *Le Monde*, whose main character's naked body is only crossed by a cape. (Quite poetically, anagramming the word *'oiseaux'* will take us to the only two cards beside *l'Impératrice* and *l'Empereur* that also show a bird). Pressed to decide between *Le Monde* and *Le Toille*, we could remember that *l'Empereur* is an anagram for *'merle pure'* (pure blackbird), which would take us to the blackbird in *Le Toille*. 'Imperatris' (as the card is named in Jean Dodal's tarot) is anagram for 'Marie strip'. Isn't that woman in *Le Toille* the very same empress who got rid of her clothes? Our choice seems obvious then.

If we start a sequence with *Le Pandu*, we notice that his hair is, naturally, upside down. The French word for 'hair' is *'cheveux'*, which is an anagram for *'chu vexé'*. *'Vexé'* is the past participle of the verb *'vexer'*, which means 'to torment' and it is usually applied to someone who is subject to an abuse of power. *'Chu'* is the past participle of the verb *'choir'*, which translates as 'falling', as in loosing balance, usually by an object's own weight. We know that the iconography of *Le Pandu* takes us to the Italian *'pitture infamanti'* or 'shame paintings'. Being hanged upside-down is a punishment for treason. Like an object taken down by its own weight, the man hanging upside-down brought his downfall to himself. So, here we have, hidden in *Le Pandu's* hair, a whole description of his circumstances!

If *Le Pandu's* hair is our 'loose brick', where in the tarot do we find him again? Look at the sun on the upper right corner of *La Maison Dieu*. The sun's rays looks like *Le Pandu's* hair. The sun is literally (ab)using all his power to make the tower fall, and with it, the two characters whose posture remind us of *Le Pandu*. Are those two people also being punished? In that case, *Le Pandu* is anagram for *'pal nude'* or *'pal nu'*, a naked branch, like the one we see in the *As de Bastons:* a club used to 'come down' on someone (like a ton of, loose, bricks), just like the powers of Heaven are coming down on that tower. In our little pataphysical game, the Ace de Batons would be the card that unites *Le Pandu* with *La Maison Dieu*.

An encore?

Le Diable is anagram for *'la bide'*, 'the belly'. (We must remember that, in the Marseille tarot, *Le Diable* has a face on his belly). In French, *"avoir un gros bide"* would mean "to have a large belly", which could send us to *Le Toille*, whose belly certainly shows, or to *La Papesse*, who in the Jean Dodal tarot is named *La Pances*. These choices would lead us into a completely different path that if we remember how, in French, *"avoir mal au bide"* would mean "to have an upset stomach". *Le Diable* certainly has a sick belly! Which other character in the tarot could be said to have an upset stomach? We must remember that *L'Ermite* carries a lantern. Have you ever wondered where is he going so late at night? In Latin, the bearer of the lantern was the *Lanternarius*, a word that conceals in it the word *latrines*. *L'Ermite* could be a man who goes into the night carrying a lantern, not so much to find God but to squat like a dog. We can actually see in his face that he is in a hurry!

This being a science of the circumstantial, we can now notice how some French dictionaries propose *'bagatelle'* (trifle, and object of little importance) as a synonym for *'lanterne'*. Just as, in Italian, *Le Fou* is called *Il Matto*, *Le Bateleur* is know as *Il Bagatto*. *Le Bateleur* (*le Bas – une bagatelle – the leurre*) would be the link between *Le Diable* and *L'Ermite*.

(Interestingly, the final sequence reminds us of Urs Graf's *Mendicant Friar Lead by the Devil* from 1512, which illustrates how, sometimes, appearances can be deceiving, and those who preach against a sin most vehemently are often the ones committing it). Perhaps *L'Ermite's* mystical airs (L'Ermite = *air myth*) are simply due to constipation.

Self-imposed rules and constrains are alternative forms of randomness. (We were inspired to create anagrams for literal words describing details in the cards by Grasset d'Orcet's methodology to read images (*Œuvres décryptées*). Grasset d'Orcet takes the gesture in a different direction, since he would always derive his decoding from the homophonies hinted by the words when they are pronounced. We chose a more 'graphic' method to allude, with letters, at the dynamics of anagramming the trump cycle into new sequences of cards. Choosing one detail in a card and anagramming the (French) word for that detail, so the resulting anagram would take us to a detail on another card, is just another way of using chance to craft cartomantic narratives. Similar results can also be reached by following the visual symmetries in the cards. *Le Pandu's* bounded hands would take us to *Le Diable*, his bent knee would take us to *l'Empereur*, his yellow hair would take us to the sun's yellow rays on *La Maison Dieu*, the green poles would take us to the *Ace de Batons*, and his shirt would take us to *Le Bateleur*.

From a visual point of view, the Marseille tarot functions as a hypertext: each image is full of 'loose bricks', and each one of them gives us a glimpse of another image. Given the visual nature of the tarot, we must expand Roussel's aim of arriving at one "unforeseen creation due to phonetic combinations", to include visual symmetries and patterns. Our goal is to arrive at an "unforessen" sequence of cards due to verbal play, visual symmetry and the synonymy of gestures (making pataphysics a *patois physique*). If the above choices seem arbitrary, then they will be in accordance with our "science of the circumstantial". No one can accuse us of claiming we have found the tarot's hidden message. If anything, we could be blamed for finding many secrets that weren't there in the first place!

Our aim is not to arrive at an ultimate truth, but to stop, albeit briefly, at an exception made true. Those who consult the Marseille tarot must regard any narrative generated while following this methodology as an answer to a question not yet asked. Moreover, the perfect answer for what hasn't yet been asked is in fact an anagram for its own question, and definitive proof of its accuracy. Such answer shouldn't leave us other choice but to match its features with the correspondent inquiry, even if that means changing altogether our original source of consternation. We can only know our reasons for consulting the tarot after the fact, so the ultimate objective of our inquiry would be to establish the grounds for inquiring in the first place. Instead of using a sequence of cards to arrive at some form of meaning, meaning-making will be the means through which we arrive at a sequence of cards, in a process that would have the Marseille tarot shuffling itself. As a result, we could have what is imaginary in our reality mirroring the imaginary solutions posed by this pataphysical machine (proposing an imaginary solution is a way of hinting at the imaginary nature of a problem). With our beliefs redefined as aesthetic choices, all of our life decisions will become poetic licenses, to such an extent that the Marseille tarot is already our only verifiable reality.

The Tarot: A Gestvral Langvage for the Common Man

Presence is meaning.
To the left, remembrance, to the right, l'Avenir.
Those who look straight at yov are seeing the present.
Fill yovr head with attention.
Do what the images do, not what they say.
Sit passively, stand receptively and walk actively.
Embody yovr destination.
Dvel with the sword, bvild with the wand,
offer a cvp, plant a coin.
Let the hands show yovr intention.
Forget what red is and notice what is red,
stand on a nvmber as yov wovld on a hill,
strip down to yovr armor;
for what tvrns gold into lead also tvrns salt into svgar,
what one step fvlfills another covld encvmber
and what yov wear wears yov down.
Know an image by its friends:
the deepest trvths hide in the obviovs.

(Note: Like the student who devours countless books on the tarot and still feels thirsty, the letter U has a blunt edge. No matter how much information it holds, it is never ready to pour that knowledge back into the world. That is why, following Jean Noblet's example, all the letters U in the above text have been turned into letters V. Those of you with a sharp edge will find in it all the necessary keys to decode the Marseille tarot's gestural language.)

Seven Ways to Learn Tarot

1.
grind the cards into a fine powder and snort it
half of it should go to the left nostril
half of it should go to the right nostril

2.
on Monday, give yourself an intravenous shot of Titanium white: 1cc
on Tuesday, give yourself an intravenous shot of Ivory black: 1 cc
on Wednesday, give yourself an intravenous shot of Cadmium red: 1 cc
on Thursday, give yourself an intravenous shot of Ultramarine blue: 1 cc
on Friday, give yourself an intravenous shot of Cadmium yellow: 1 cc
on Saturday, give yourself an intravenous shot of SAP green: 1 cc
on Sunday, drink lots of water.

3.
load nonsense into your hard-drive

WARNING: believing in the literal value of a myth transforms it into a lie

4.
learn by heart:

"You have a need for other people to like and admire you, and yet you tend to be critical of yourself. While you have some personality weaknesses you are generally able to compensate for them. You have considerable unused capacity that you have not turned to your advantage. Disciplined and self-controlled on the outside, you tend to be worrisome and insecure on the inside. At times you have serious doubts as to whether you have made the right decision or done the right thing. You prefer a certain amount of change and variety and become dissatisfied when hemmed in by restrictions and limitations. You also pride yourself as an independent thinker, and do not accept others' statements without satisfactory proof. But you have found it unwise to be too frank in revealing yourself to others. At times you are extroverted, affable, and sociable, while at other times you are introverted, wary, and reserved. Some of your aspirations tend to be rather unrealistic."

and parrot it no matter which cards you get

5.
sleep with your tarot
sit on your tarot
take it to McDonald's and buy it a Happy Meal

6.
write each image's name on a suppository
but only if you are *really* committed

7.
do what the image does
not what the image says

Visual Teaching: The Trumps

TAROT

Robert Pinsky's poem 'Rhyme' from his book *Gulf Music* starts with this stanza:

Air an instrument of the tongue,
The tongue an instrument
Of the body, the body
An instrument of spirit,
The spirit a being of the air.

I find it to be a perfect description of the way vowels and consonants work together to create the shape of a word. By extension, this stanza is also a perfect example of the way trumps and pips, major and minor arcana, work together so that the tarot can talk to us.

When we say "AAAAA..." this sound made of vowels alone can create a psychological effect in us. It can resonate in us. But some times it is very hard to say what the sound is about. Even when the sound is 'working' us, it is very hard to put into words what is going on in us while listening to this sound. I feel that is what happens sometimes with the Major arcana. Depending on the level of awareness in the person looking at the tarot images, their effect may be more or less 'unpronounceable'. It is not that they don't have an effect, but that the effect may be hard to put into words, or to translate into an applicable notion. It happens often that we are all inspired, describing the breakthrough implicit in *La Maison Dieu*, for example, and we can tell by the other person's face that she is wondering "yes, yes, but, is my boyfriend going to break-up with me or what?"

Vowels are made of air, pure air. Air is as ethereal as the archetypes depicted in the tarot's trumps. That is why we say that the vowels of a word are its soul, just as the trumps in the tarot are a tool for soul-making. But as Pinsky points out in his poem, the soul needs the tongue, and the body, to be perceived. Since, physiologically speaking, consonants are obstacles we put to the air coming from our throat so the vowels can get reshaped into intelligible phonemes, we like to say that consonants are the body of a word.

Like our vowels, the trumps may need 'consonants' to qualify them. The sound of "AAAAA..." gets clearly qualified if we use a consonant to reshape it. When we say "MAAAAA..." and then "MAAAA..." again, we know what these sounds are about. There is no doubt about the way in which these sounds are working us. That is the role of the pips, or minor arcana. The pips are to the tarot what consonants are to the vowels, what the body is to the soul. They are there to qualify the trumps. They talk about health, money, romance, work... And they become especially useful when people are not ready for pure soul-making. *Temperance*, for example, could seem incomprehensible for a person, but it becomes easy to understand if we use the *Two of Coins* to qualify it. Right there, *Temperance* becomes the act of "balancing our checkbook", and the person looking at the cards can approach the principle from a tangible, albeit more limited, perspective.

We can explore any word by looking at its soul and body. This way, a word becomes more than the sum of its parts and gets turned into a meditation. In this little game, and in the game of tarot as well, it will be more useful to look at the shape of the letters than to focus on concepts. The secret is to let spontaneity regale us with a direct comprehension.

A very fortunate word to exemplify this would be the word TAROT.

TAROT is:

Soul: AO

Body: TRT

The letter A resembles the stand of *Le Bateleur*, while the letter O suggests the mandala in *Le Monde*. (The mandorla, dear friend, is that floral ellipse that encircles the naked woman in the middle of the card). The soul of the word TAROT will therefore describe the tarot's first and last trumps.

What about the body of the word? As a structure, TRT suggests a journey (letter R) whose destination is the same as its departure point. Between these two letters T we have ARO. The letter R suggests the forward motion of *Le Fov*, communicating the letter A with the letter O. In other words, ARO would describe *Le Fov's* pilgrimage, from 'here and now', as depicted by *Le Bateleur*, to the state of transcendence depicted in *Le Monde*. The fact that this journey is framed by the two letters T is quite relevant, since it seems to suggest that *Le Fov's* pilgrimage never ends. We travel far away to end up where we began.

Maybe what matters are these few things we understand along the way. Sometimes we use the tarot to raise difficult questions, not to answer them.

LE FOV

Lets turn the card's name into images.

Let's imagine that there are two axes, a vertical one representing a sense of being, and an horizontal one representing a sense of becoming. These axes unite "above" with "below" and "past" with "future". Let's take the most minimal shape in our alphabet, the letter I. It is made from one single stroke. The letter I would represent the individual. Now, let's assume that our sense of being gets reshaped by our sense of becoming. That is, when the vertical axis represented by the letter I is activated horizontal-wise, we have the letter I reshaping itself to form all the other letters in the alphabet. This way, by understanding the 'motion' that took place from the original vertical stroke to become a letter, we have a narrative we can follow, turning any word or name into a meditation.

When the letter I breaks apart to become receptive to the ground, we have a letter A. When the letter I grows arms to grab the world it creates the letter B. If the letter I curves itself, forming a letter C, it becomes receptive towards the future. The letter D is a letter I that became pregnant. The letter E is a letter I expanding on three parallel levels that we can equate with the mind, the heart, and the body. The letter F is a letter E whose physical development, its connection to the ground, isn't complete, and runs the risk of falling down due to excessive idealism.

The letter G is egocentric. Can you see how it is always pointing to itself? The letter H resembles a staircase, dividing above and below; but it could also be seen as two letters I joining forces so we can climb up. The letter J is always running the risk of getting hooked to the ground. Can you see why? The letter K stands like a martial artist, both receptive and active towards the right, while keeping its back straight. (In our narrative, the right can be understod as the future).

The letter L is a letter I that only expands on a physical plane. The letter M seems like two letters I holding hands while some other times it looks like a sexy woman with a v-neck sweater. The letter N is elastic. Two letters I guard a proper distance thanks to that diagonal line separating them, but diagonals are always dynamic and we suspect that sometimes these two letters I may get closer than others. The letter O is a letter I who closed itself to become whole. The O says "Being and becoming are one single thing". The letter P is an F whose heart and mind got fused. The idealist became a champion. The letter Q got some vices from the letter J, or perhaps, it is telling us that wholeness is but a moment. All eggs must be hatched.

Can you see how the letter R resembles a train, always rrrrrruning forward? Can you see how the letter S slithers from above to below, connecting both planes with a flickery line? The letter T found its intellectual limit, while the letter U is intellectually limitless because it is always receptive. But the letter V has an advantage over the letter U: it is receptive to above, while active below. The W puzzles me. Are these two letter Vs joining forces or competing against each other? Beware of the letter X. It is receptive to each one of the four corners, and therefore, it can realize itself by becoming a center point, or expand forever in all directions. The letter Y is a letter I whose head is split open, and I would like to ask the letter Z if there is real need of keeping a distance between heaven and earth.

This is a game, and the only rule is to look again. I will start with Le Fov because he is going somewhere, and by doing so he offers to take us there too. Perhaps this pilgrim is walking straight to Le Bateleur, perhaps not. In any case, this card is as good as any other to start playing with shapes and letters. Words are composed by vowels and consonants. Vowels emerge from the guttural sound our breath produces, while consonants are created when our lips, tongue, and mouth put a resistance to that guttural sound. Biologist Luc Bigé wants to imagine that, since vowels are made of breath, while consonants are physical limits we impose on that breath, vowels can be seen as the soul of words, while consonants would be the body of the word. I find that simile useful. When we breath some vowels over a few consonants, a word happens.

LE FOV

In LE FOV we have

A soul: E O

And a body: L F V

The soul of Le Fov's name is composed by the letters E O, inviting us to think that we achieve wholeness (letter O) by expanding at all three intellectual, emotional, and physical levels (letter E). It makes us remember that the soul of LE MONDE is conformed by the letters E O E. When we place Le Fov and Le Monde together we can see how our pilgrim aims at the ideal represented by that woman in the center of the mandala. The Fool's aim is to inseminate the World. Look at E O. Don´t they look like Le Fov trying to embrace Le Monde? In Le Fov, E and O are saying: "expand your intellect, expand your heart, expand your body and you will be whole". In Le Monde, E O E are saying: "once you have expanded and become whole, expand again". If Le Fov and Le Monde join souls we get: E O E O E, a rhythm that sounds like the worry-free chant of an infant.

And now, can you see how much the L F V feel like Le Fov? The body of his name fits the character like a glove. The L talks about expanding through the ground, just like that man who is eternally walking. If we look at Le Fov's face we can see the letter F acting as a guiding principle in it: in the letter F the heart and the mind move forward. L and F suggests a disconnection between Le Fov's upper and lower body. It is not exactly that what is happening in the card? His feet walk on one reality while his mind walks in another one. We find no signs in his face of the pain the wild creature is inflicting on Le Fov's genitals. Finally, the letter V is there to tell Le Fov: "Be opened-up". Just as E O are saying "expand and be whole", L F V contains a simple message: "walk with your feet, feel with your heart, think with your mind, trust inspiration".

BATELEUR

Poet Billy Collins wrote: "When a metaphor strikes us powerfully with its originality and its aptness, we almost feel that a new neuronal path has been created in us, that a previously dormant synapse has been activated. Insofar as such a metaphor rewires our way of perceiving, we experience a breakthrough in the usual categories of thought."

In our game with letters, we aren't decoding any secret. We are just playing with shapes to see where they will take us, knowing that they will only take us as far as the image itself will allow. The image on the card becomes the foreground of the card's name, so we can explore the rhymes and resonances that occur between text and image. If we indulge in this silly little game of reading the names of the cards as images, we run the risk of finding something we aren't looking for. That's just what we want. How much can we understand about a card by looking at its name? How many times can we find our Bateleur in the word 'bateleur'? And then, what else will we find there?

If we remain loyal to the idea of vowels being the soul of a word while consonants are the body of the word, we have this:

The soul of the word 'bateleur' is: AEEU

The body of the word 'bateleur' is: BTLR

AEEU: The letter A is the quintessential representation of Le Bateleur: an individual standing on the ground, the legs wide apart anchoring the body, the head pointing toward the sky, and the solar plexus, represented by the horizontal stroke right in the middle of the letter, steadily anchoring the whole structure. Strong balance, solid instinct and a sharp head: that's our magician. The letter A is the first letter in our alphabet, just as Le Bateleur is the first trump. Both share the same body posture and the same position within their systems. Le Bateleur is all body, all presence in the material realm. But AEEU is an interesting structure that suggests an evolution, taking us from being receptive to the ground (letter A) to being receptive to the sky (letter U). Right in the middle, the expansive letter E gets doubled, as if suggesting the repetitive work of the artist who has to practice his sleights until they become second nature. In other words, the soul of the word AEEU seems to be telling us "repetition turns practice into insight". It is through the smallest things that we reach transcendence.

Now look at this: BTLR. Only the letter T suggest stillness, while the B, the L and the R face right, suggesting a motion forward. Le Bateleur is always on the move! His table never remains at the same spot for too long.

Look at the first and last of these four letters: BTLR. The letter B is full of possibilities, like two milky breasts, like two protruding eyes wanting to see it all, like our two arms holding a treasure against our chest. But the B will go nowhere unless it becomes an R. The R moves forward, "RRRRRRRRRRRRRR", by letting go of one leg. Is it not precisely this which happens with that coin our Bateleur is holding in his right hand? The coin can appear or it can vanish, but it can't remain still in the hand forever or the hand will freeze, making any further act of legerdemain impossible. Money, like blood, must circulate. L and R are a deconstructed B.

And the letter T… It looks like an individual wearing a hat, just like our Bateleur. Hats are vertical limits. Hats protect us from the rain or the sun, but they also prevent body heat from abandoning us through the head. Nothing can come in, nothing can get out. Joseph Beuys wore a felt hat, hoping to become a hare. The metaphor of the hat-as-personality, the hat-as-mask, is very prevalent in our society: "put on your thinking cap", "I wear many hats", "the hat makes the man"… Our Bateleur seems to be wearing a hat that is too big or too heavy for his head, which seems to be shrinking. Maybe the T is there to remind us that heaven is a hat.

Le Bateleur's hat imposes a vertical limit that suggests, by default, a horizontal expansion. "Beware of what you wear" – the BLTR seems to be saying – "because what we pretend to be, we become."

LA PAPESSE, LE PAPE

Our game is very close to *la langue des oiseaux,* the language of the birds, without claiming to actually employ it. The only certainty we have about *la langue des oiseaux* is that it invites us to imagine that things can just be what they seem to be. I like Jean-Claude Flornoy's definition of *la langue des oiseaux* as a language that functions through "spontaneity and direct comprehension". But the true intent and secrets of this language are lost to us. We have forgotten it. Forgetting is a way of dying, and we can say that the language of the birds is a dead tongue. Here, we are trying to revive it a little by making one major shift: we ignore the sound of the letters. In our view, they have become graphic objects. Why? Because the letter AA that a Frenchman pronounces is not the same as pronounced by an Englishman, or the same letter A a Spaniard pronounces; but all these letters A look the same. That gives us enough common ground for playing with the shapes of letters, turning words into meditations.

PAPESSE is: soul: AEE, and body: PPSS

PAPE is: soul: AE, and body PP

Can you see how much softer La Papesse feels?

The main difference between the names of these two cards – what La Papesse has and Le Pape is missing – is that double SS for a few moments. If we follow its shape with our finger over and over and over we are driven into a sort of trance. Moving from below to above and from above to below, the letter S connects both realms in a fluid two-way dialogue. If the S talks about a vertical exchange of information, a double S suggests a reverberation akin to the act of praying. This repetitive gesture drives our mind into a meditative state that is conducive to making analogies.

Le Pape has lost La Papesse's SS and with it, he has lost his connection to heaven. His kingdom is certainly of this world. SS suggests that La Papesse inhabits a vertical empire while Le Pape inhabits a horizontal one. PAPE is PP + AE. PP evokes war banners, while the A and the E are talking about establishing territories and expanding them. These letters seem to be saying: "take my insignias, claim a ground for me, expand my empire". Is not this exactly what the figure's hand suggests in its blessing? Le Pape's right hand gives us a "go ahead" signal. Pape, PapeSSE... the addition of these last three letters comes to soften the male 'pop' present in the masculine version of the word. Our focus – these two letters S suggest – shoudn't be forward but upward.

When we compare the soul of these two words: AE for Le Pape and AEE for La Papesse, we see how La Papesse suggests a further expansion. While Le Pape prays where all can see him, La Papesse prays alone. While La Papesse waits, Le Pape seems to know. The words 'papesse' and 'pape' leave us with the feeling that it is better to experience the learning than to learn the experience.

Little by little we see how everything in the tarot expresses the tension between being and becoming. The double S reinforces a question: if there is an above, and there is a below, who is above La Papesse? We don´t know. This is a good thing, since not knowing is the root of wonder. Who is above Le Pape? No one. That much we know. The cards clearly state that he stands above his two acolytes. Who is above La Papesse? An angel, perhaps, although I would like to believe that angels are sudden thoughts.

The conclusion of our little game will always be the point at which we decide to stop playing.

L EMPERATRISE – LEMPEREVR – LEMPERANCE

León Battista Alberti wrote: "When the men painted in the picture outwardly demonstrate the movement of their souls as clearly as possible, the story will move the spectator's souls in turn". Something similar can be read in Jules Lubbock's *Storytelling in Christian Art. From Giotto to Donatello:* "We do not simply take in stories and absorb their lessons about the world. Rather, when we read about Zeus seducing a young woman, we involuntarily imitate his feelings and behavior." Saint Agustine would define that as *verba visibilia*, that is, an image as visible speech. Because it is a set of narrative pictures, the tarot exists at the limit of what can be said with words. If we want to understand the true advice hidden in the tarot, we would have to write-off most of what has been said about it. After we have taken our ocultist's helmet off, we will be able to see the tarot images with the naked eye and discover that each image's true meaning has been encrypted in its character's *posture*.

In our game with letters, we find three cards whose names look extremely similar. We look at L EMPERATRISE and immediately notice the similarity between her name and LEMPEREVR. This isn't surprising, since they are of course a couple. But then, we are puzzled to find a third card sharing very much the same name: LEMPERANCE. Why has TEMPERANCE been re-baptised? Jean-Claude Flornory would suggest that by writing an L at the beginning of the name, Jean Noblet was giving away the fact that he was a *master companion*. In any case, let us thank the master for bringing to light an interesting dynamic that will help us understand how our images are 'hiding' their advice in plain sight.

If we place these images in sequence: L EMPERATRISE–LEMPEREVR–LEMPERANCE, L EMPERATRISE and LEMPEREVR look like a bourgeois couple who sit lazy and fat in their living room while LEMPERANCE, the maid, fixes them a drink. In fact, the eagles on the shields of L EMPERATRISE and LEMPEREVR remind us a bit of Chaucer's eagles in the "Parliament of the Fowls": two of the same species refuse to mate. Why? When we look closer, a little soap opera emerges: L EMPERATRISE is furious, since LEMPEREVR only has eyes for LEMPERANCE.

L EMPERATRISE, LEMPEREVR and LEMPERANCE share the root LEMPER. Look at the vowels: one letter E chases the other letter E, just like LEMPEREVR tries to charm LEMPERANCE by offering her his scepter. L EMPERATRISE stands behind, like the letter L, firmly holding her ground.

We will get back to the rest of the letters in LEMPER shortly.

The remaining portions of these cards' names flirt with us. It is impossible not to unite them into one word. Rearranged, ATRISE EVR ANCE ends up being A TRI SEVERANCE, as in a triple separation!

We are about to feed the evening news with some juicy drama...

But here is where we need to pay attention and obtain the advice the cards conceal. In a way that's suspiciously similar to what we see in LAMOVREVX: our little sequence shows the three roles a person could play in a love triangle, and it also suggests a possible way to play each role for the benefit of all involved. One could be the cheated party, like L EMPERATRISE. In this case, the figure is telling us: *"Be strong and hold onto what's yours"*. Can you see how she is doing precisely that? One could be the cheater, like LEMPEREVR, who leans back with his hand on his belt, as if to say: *"Control yourself. Cross your legs so you cannot jump forward. Keep your pants on!"* Or one can be the third party, like LEMPERANCE, whose posture seems to be telling us: *"Stay away from temptation, and if you feel passion barking closer, cool it off!"*

See how the tarot's characters are advice in disguise?

We can see the effects of following this advice in a happy resolution: LEMPERANCE is the last image on our right. Back to the root LEMPER, the last letter on our right is the R, who seems to be about to take off, leaving M and P, this is, Mater and Pater, mother and father, alone. Perhaps then the letter P will see itself as a flag, ready to conquer those mountains the letter M represents.

LAMORT - LAMOVREVX

Why are we dealing with Death and Love at the same time? Because if we look closer, we notice how both LAMORT and LAMOVREVX have the word AMOR, love, hiding at their core. In the case of LAMOVREVX, this seems to make sense. After all, this card depicts the challenge of knowing where our true passions lie. We will have to enact LAMORT's scything motion to understand that his work is also an act of love, since it is he who does the hardest job, the one that needs to be done but no one wants to do.

LAMORT is: Soul: AO and Body: LMRT

LAMOVREVX is: Soul: AOVEV and Body: LMRX

LAMORT's soul, AO, seems like an exact rendition of the character in the card. By being in total harmony with the earth, reaping what it has produced (letter A), the skeleton attains wholeness (letter O). We see a similar structure in LAMOVREVX's soul, AOVEV, but in this case the letter A (which mimics the exact posture of the Lover's legs) and the letter O stand in conjunction with VEV. VEV is an assemblage that bears a strong resemblance to the image in the card. The letter E stands between two letters V, both of them attractive, both promising an open path to heaven. But there is more here than meets the eye. In fact, if we pay close attention, we see how these three letters are letting us into a little secret: the lover has made his choice already. Can you see how the letter E throws its arms towards the letter V on our right? Can you see how this gesture is present in the card's image? Look at the lover's left hand! It is already on third base!

Let's look at the body of these two words. Both LAMORT and LAMOVREVX share LMR, that is, the certainty that any expansion we attempt in this world (letter L) would be fruitless unless we find an object of passion (letter M, seen as two letters I mirroring each other or holding hands). Only then will our expansion in the world accelerate (letter R). But the truly relevant detail here is found in the difference between these two words. LAMORT ends with a T, suggesting a horizontal line broken towards the earth. Again, the letters evoke the act of reaping! LAMOVREVX ends with an X, a letter that resembles the alleged crossroad on which the card's main character seems to be standing. But, as we already saw in the letter E, it is possible that this crossroad is illusory: the card could be reminding us the fact that 'confusion' doesn't exist, but is just a game we play when we know what we should do and don't want to face the consequences.

LECHARIOT

Whatever happens in our lives is of little importance. What matters is how we tell the story of what has happened to us. That is why an old proverb says "Don't trust the teller. Trust the tale". Truth is not what is given to us, but what we receive. Let us look at the name written on the card named LECHARIOT. Pursuing our little game, how much of that charioteer, his vehicle, the horses and their tale, can we find in such a word?

LECHARIOT is:

Body: LCHRT

Soul: EAIO

In the word's body, the letter L indicates a departure filled with hubris. LECHARIOT has set out to conquer the physical world. The letter C opens like a bag that lets its cat out: this cat is a letter H. Can you see how that letter H is LECHARIOT itself? The letter H signals the vertical structure that gives LECHARIOT its shape. A horizontal line right in the middle of the rectangular structure separates above from below, just as a similar flesh-colored line separates the charioteer from the two horses. The letter H, right at the heart of the word, reminds us that we can't run a marathon if our brain has been severed from our spine. That is why, no matter how fast LECHARIOT runs (letter R), its accomplishments will be severely limited (letter T).

(Curiously, in the Jean Dodal tarot, our chariot is named LE CHARIOR, ending in R and not in T. It is a good thing that Freudian slips hadn't been invented at the time. Otherwise we would have to talk about the "penis envy" the letter T would suffer when compared to the letter R. There is no doubt that LECHARIOR moves faster than LECHARIOT, with that letter R at the very end, running forward with the intensity of a locomotive!)

The soul of this word leaves no doubt. A horse (letter E) stands on his hind legs, trying to jump over an obstacle (letter A). By forcing himself to surmount the obstacle, the horse runs the risk of getting impaled (letter I) or of falling into a bottomless pit (letter O). The soul of this word bears the imprint of LECHARIOT's downfall: arrogance can defeat any army, even before the battle starts. After all, LECHARIOT's wheels are stuck on the ground. LECHARIOT can neither jump nor detach its progress from the rotation of the earth. Perhaps it is there to remind us that we can ride a wave as long as we are willing to follow it wherever it takes us. Riding the wave with elegance transforms us into masters, but demands humility. WE are our own masters, not the wave's master. We constantly ought to remind ourselves that we don't own the wave, but we can embellish it, just as it is our duty to embellish all our tales about the waves we have ridden before.

IVSTICE

Let us now look at IVSTICE, and feel the urge to "right some wrongs". Why is it that in all our images' names the letter V replaces the letter U? Shouldn't we simply write JUSTICE? When we compare the letter U to the letter V, we understand that we could, but should not.

Why?

Because, although both the letter U and the letter V are receptive to heaven, only the letter V is active towards earth. While the letter V acts like a funnel, decanting inspiration into action, the letter U is like a cup that gets filled with inspiration but keeps it contained, preventing it from impregnating the ground. Developing that metaphor, allow me to bluntly suggest that the letter U mimics a condom, while the letter V is hanging unrestrained. Referring to what we said earlier, the letter V reminds us that *Ingenium Non Valet Nisi Facta Valebunt* ("Our wit is worthless unless we have the will to work").

So, let's keep the word IVSTICE as it is. Notice that the word's soul is IVIE, while the word's body is STC.

Can you see how STC portrays IVSTICE itself? In one 'hand' the letter T holds a letter S. Given the natural motion of the letter S, connecting above and below, we can see it representing the sword, whose handle points to the ground, while its tip reaches towards heaven. In the other 'hand' the letter T holds a letter C. IVSTICEO, the letter C is always waiting to be filled, just like the plates on a scale. We may even go so far as to say that the letter

C is incomplete until it has been filled. There is something else worth noticing here: the balance between directions that is suggested by STC. While the letter S implies a vertical direction, the letter C opens to the right, and evokes a horizontal one. Justices invite our sense of being to always inform our sense of becoming.

And how do we do that? Well, IVIE indicates an important shift. IVI also resembles our crowned lady: the letter V intercedes between two letters I. These three letters take us back to the idea of IVSTICE as a mediator. But then we have the letter E, indicating an expansion taking place on three levels: physical, emotional, and intellectual. How can this be accomplished? By resonating with the horizontal direction suggested by the letter C, the letter E reminds us that we shouldn't get stuck in other people's conundrums. With its arms and legs reaching out, the letter E is telling us: "If you are given the power to rule over other peoples' lives, get out of there!", because the most important kind of justice has nothing to do with judging others. On the contrary, ultimate justice consists in giving ourselves what we deserve.

IVSTCE uses her sword to cut what she doesn't need and then uses the scale to make sense of what is left.

LERMITE

"I believe the 21st century will be a world without art in the sense that we have it now. It will be a world without objects, where the human being can be on such a high level of consciousness and has such a strong mental state that he or she can transmit thoughts and energy to other people, without needing objects in between... [The public and artist] will just sit or stand, like the Samurai in old Japan, looking at each other and transmitting energy. This is the future world I see as an artist: a non-objective world" (Marina Abramovic).

The tarot presents us with a set of mental operations that we can use to change the way we think about something. If we accept each one of the tarot characters as real beings that 'stand' before us, inviting us to mimic their actions, we will find ourselves enacting Abramovic's 'prediction'.

If we stand mirroring LERMITE, with a lamp in our left hand and a cane in our right, we become the letter L that begins this word. In front of us, the lantern's light shows us where we came from. We know what we have experienced. Behind us, the lantern's light casts our own shadow, obscuring the future. Can you see how, just as the letter L is a letter I projecting its shadow on the ground, there is nothing behind LERMITE? The card shows a clear yellow path in front of him, but a blank space behind. This suggests that LERMITE walks backwards, inviting us to trust that there will always be a way, even if the light of reason hasn't yet discovered it.

LERMITE is Soul: EIE and Body: LRMT

The letter I, surrounded by letters E, feels alone. All these letters E seek something out there. They chase the external world with arms outstretched like zombies, while the letter I stays silent. No matter how certain these letters E seem to be about their goals and destination, the letter I distrusts their effort knowing that, wherever they insist on standing, they won't leave any imprint.

Look at the word's body: LRMT. United, the letters L and T would create a square, a solid figure in which RM can resonate and create an echo. And what is RM? Some things cannot be explained but only experienced. RRRRR… and MMMMM… are vibrant sounds. Pronounce them and you will immediately feel lifted. These are cathedral sounds. Sounds that we can't hear if we run ahead, but that will re-build us if we stop and listen.

LA ROVE DE FORTVNE

Each word is a vault ready to reward those who unlock it with a message. Many times, separating the vowels from the consonants in the title of a tarot card will lead us to the discovery of the image's workings. We only have to look at the vowels in LA ROVE DE FORTVNE to realize how true this is: A OVE E OVE. See what is happening there? The vowels conform a repetitive rhythm that reveals the main feature of the image: change is a constant cycle.

The vowels present us with two rounds of that cycle. The first round is preceded by the letter A, while the second round starts with the letter E. What is the difference? The letter A has a vertical emphasis. It moves from a broad base to a narrow point at the top, like an arrow. The contrary is true of the letter E, whose emphasis is horizontal: three horizontal stripes move right from a vertical pole on the left. The letter A reminds us of the little king on top of the wheel. A king who can be easily overthrown if he insists on remaining upright. We either change or break. On the other hand, the letter E reminds us of the two animals going up and down around he wheel; creatures whose bodies have become so fixed in this rotation device that we can't tell where they end and where the wheel begins. In other words, these two rounds of an infinite cycle: OVE... OVE... OVE... suggest that we need to become movement, so we can be part of change without being broken by it.

No matter how firmly we stand, the earth is always spinning.

The A has to become an E. We need to understand the rhythm of the world if we want to dance with it, for we cannot impose our rhythm on the world. Once we have understood this, the consonants in the name of this image start making sense. They are a parade of trumps going around Fortune's wheel: L R D FRTN. There we can see Le Fov and Lempereur. We also see Le Pendu and Le Soleil, and even more. Can you tell which is which? Can you identify the other three letters?

FORCE

People in the Middle Ages hoped that painting was capable of "revealing the invisible by means of the visible". The fact that we aren't medieval people doesn't prevent us from also wanting a peek into the unseen. Tarot images are little miracles, unexpected apparitions that shake us from our day-to-day trance and startle us, elated, into a place where reality is no more. In this way, tarot images allow us to experience notions that cannot be put into words.

When we look at the word FORCE, we find in particular how the progression from the letter O to the letter C resembles the main action in the image: a woman holds a lion's mouth open. If we see the letter O as being closed, we can perceive the letter C as an open letter O. It is interesting to notice that if we look from the F to the E and back again, we will also see the E as a letter F that opens up. Perhaps the letter E is a letter F whose jaw has dropped! This transition from F to E mirrors the transition from O to C. In other words, the letter F becomes a letter E so the letter O can become a letter C.

What does all this mean?

We may never know, but we can tell what it might imply. In this case, these letters seem to suggest: "An individual who evolves only at an intellectual and spiritual level (letter F) remains closed to reality (letter O), but when the individual opens up to let reality in (letter C), his intellectual and spiritual growth leads to material expansion (letter E)".

In other words, all our theories and beliefs only matter if they help us to overcome our fears.

And, what about that letter R we have been ignoring?

Well, given the presence of our lion, a lion that we see twice in the tarot (active in FORCE, and receptive in LE MONDE), we can safely assume that the letter R is the lion's roar, lying dormant, safely concealed in the middle of the word, waiting for us to let it out.

LE PENDV

Our game of tarot is based on spontaneity. That is why, when a friend proposed to turn LE PENDV around and look at his name upside down, I knew I had to oblige. He was acting like Le Fov, always ready to leave us breathless with his sudden inspiration.

When we look at the word PENDV upside down, we discover a theme of treason running through the whole word. This recalls the alleged Medieval origin of the image as depicting a punishment for traitors. The reversed V feels like a heartless letter A. The reversed letter D feels like a C which wants to swallow a letter I. That reversed D resembles a crocodile, its mouth open, with one of those cleaning birds inside. Can the bird really trust the crock's jaws to remain open? In the letter N, two letters I keep their distance, always suspicious of each other. The letter N suggests an accordion-like movement, similar to the 'dance' of a spy shadowing his target. The letter E seems like a letter I that has been stabbed three times in the back. Finally, the letter P always feels like a letter F whose passion and intellect have fused. The P is a letter I pregnant with high notions. An idealist. In this particular case, we look at the reversed letter P and realize that it is hanging head-down like our PENDV. In other words, the little story in these letters would be something like: "A heartless man, wanting to take over another's man life, watched from a distance until the time was right to stab him in the back, three times! He then buried the corpse upside down."

Quite a plot!

If we sober up just a little – but just a little – we can see that these letters concern the worst kind of treason: self-betrayal. In our obsession with material stability (letter V reversed) we get jealous of our neighbour's possessions (letter D reversed, giving us C+ I). The greener we see the grass on his side of the fence (letter N), the sharper the sting of all our false expectations (letter E reversed). I say 'false' because our neighbour's expectations shouldn't be ours. We owe it to ourselves to craft our own definition of success. We want what others have, we try to live other peoples' lives, and life manages to have us stuck with our heads buried in the ground (letter P reversed). We can use that situation to look at the world from our very own perspective, and hopefully reconnect with our roots.

And when we look at the word PENDV upside down something else happens: we are in fact releasing our PENDV. He is upright now, floating! He seems to be quoting the Latin proverb: POST NUBILA PHOEBUS: "After the clouds comes the sun".

LE DIABLE (To my friend Christian Scheidemann)

Who is this character that pops out like a Jack-in-the-box, throwing the little toy soldier off the window ledge and causing so much uneasiness in those who look at him?

DIABLE is:

Body: DBL, Soul: IAE

In English, the Devil without the initial D becomes EVIL. Evil is the anagram of LIVE. LIVE begins with the letter L and ends with the letter E: the word takes us from a mindless and spiritless path (letter L) to a balanced expansion involving both the physical body and the emotional and intellectual centers (letter E). In between these two we see the individual (letter I) making itself receptive to heaven and active towards earth (letter V).

In our game of shapes we see how the same letters arranged in a different order lead us to a completely different reflection .

EVIL starts with the letter E, which can be seen as a letter I that has grown arms and legs so it can embrace the future. One can imagine that the letter expands at three levels: material, emotional and intellectual. The letter V is receptive to heaven, and active to the ground, like a funnel that focuses all intentions and ideas and transforms them into action. The letter I represents the individual and is the simplest letter in the alphabet, made by one single stroke. The letter I, the perfect individual, comes to be when our expansion (E) leads to effective action in reality (V). But then we have the letter L. Maybe the L is a letter I that casts a shadow on the ground. And, what would that shadow be? Back to the letter E, the L would signal an expansion that occurs only on a physical level, or in other words, living without awareness. So, yes, EVIL is a way to LIVE indeed.

It seems that there is no way to escape that L and its shadow, present in as many renditions of the word Diable as we can think of: the English DEVIL, the Spanish DIABLO, the Italian DIAVOLO. In the Italian, we are surprised to find two letters O, L is present in all of these languages! (By the way, did you notice how the words 'two open' also have two eyes wide open right between them, looking at us? Our little game is infinite!) Even the German for for devil: TEUFEL ends with this same letter L. '*Teufel*' is in fact an interesting word. Its soul wants to be free. EUE suggest expansion in the world and receptivity to heaven. But the word's body pulls it down: TFLT and a divorce between the mind and spirit (letter F) and the body (letter L). F L could create a very nice letter E, but that doesn´t seems to be the case here. They co-exist separately. Again, a life without awareness!

And, what about that D the word evil is missing? Since the letter D can be seen as a letter I that got pregnant, it seems to stand for the creative principle,. Therefore, a DEVIL who cannot create, but can only destroy, would certainly be EVIL. Not only that: it would also be rather flat and uninteresting, a puppet.

Our DIABLE is not like that. It has a pregnant D, ripe and ready to give birth, and two handsome breasts (the letter B). Can you see how the creature depicted in the card also has a living womb and full teats? I would love to tell you something about these two characters chained at Le Diable's feet, but I tend to ignore people wearing leather and chains suggesting two open mouths. The creature on the card also has two mouths. The letter suggests an obstacle to reaching heaven.

Compare the letters B and E. As in a "BEFORE AND AFTER" poster, the E shows a broken letter B, a letter B that has exploded, and whose energy has been released. That is what the word DIABLE suggests, the unleashed energy of the proverbial trickster, ready to stir things up a little, to have us acknowledging our creativity and keeping our eyes open.

LA MAISON DIEV

Images are miracles and they deserve to be treated accordingly. When we contemplate an image we shouldn't label it with a rational tag, as if it were a corpse we want to bag. We must let the image engage our senses so the senses can engage our mind. That mind of ours, which can heal the spirit and move the body, must interrogate the image and ask: "What are you showing me? What are you making visible?"

If there is an image from the tarot that deserves to be interrogated, it would be LA MAISON DIEV, which in the last three centuries has been transformed from a House-of-God into just a tall building.

LA MAISON DIEV is: Soul: A AIO IEV, and Body: L MSN D

In A AIO IEV, two letters A become an E and a V, but only after ignoring the allure of a void represented by the letter O. For the first letter A, becoming a letter V would imply giving itself up to heavenly inspiration: the individual becomes a funnel. For the second letter A, becoming a letter E would signify a progressive understanding of how to transform that inspiration into action in the world: the individual becomes a staircase. But this is easier said than done, since that letter O exerts such a huge attraction! As proof of this, two letters I stand around the letter O, like a schematic depiction of the previous image: LE DIABLE. In fact, we can suppose that the tower is where LE DIABLE holds his slaves captive. Just as in LE DIABLE, the characters seem to willingly accept the devil's leash, these two letters I seem to have surrendered to the letter O voluntarily. They stare, stiff and mesmerized, at the emptiness of the O, just as we have all stared at a void now and then, in one of those sparkling moments where wrong feels so right.

A flash or thunderous flame would be necessary to wake us up. We find our flame among the consonants, in the letter S, whose movement suggests a dialogue between the realms of heaven and earth. The letter S is a whip-like lighting bolt, and Jean Noblet tells us that this is a very peculiar kind of lighting, since it breaks from the tower to crack into the sky. Among the consonants we notice how the letter S stands right in the middle of a 'structure' created by the letters M and N. Each of those two letters contains two letters I separated by diagonal lines: double-layered walls holding slanted whispers. They separate the initial L, which talks about our mundane expansion, from the final D, whose pregnancy suggests our capacity to deliver ourselves to transcendence.

In other words – or in other letters – the name on this image seems to be telling us to avoid the temptation of growing stiff. From time to time, it would be healthy to break down; then, like the famous poet Rumi, we can say:

> Birds make great sky circles
> of their freedom.
> How do they learn that?
> They fall, and falling,
> They're given wings.

(Translated by Coleman Barks)

LA LVNE

We may remember fear.

We have arrived at the only card in which human characters are absent, which suggests that we are invited to *wait until it is safe to come out*. And while we wait, we may want to ask ourselves: what is really going on here? This is LA LVNE, a card we experience with our spine sending a shiver to the hairs on our back. As soon as we become aware of these hairs, which may very well have never been there before, we realize we have become werewolves, and we are howling too, just like the two dogs in the image.

Looking at an image can affect us. It does so because our thoughts are malleable. When we pour our thoughts into an image, and the image embodies these thoughts, our thoughts change. When an image accommodates our thoughts, it reshapes them. Images can change us. Images give us something to hold on to. We aren't talking about 'hope', but about a practical structure for our psyche.

Images are mental operations. They embody our intellectual processes and give us something to aspire to. When we look at Le Bateleur, for example, we don't really seek to become magicians, but we aim to stand up straight while making use of all the tools available to us. Images suggest a physicality that the mind translates into the memory of the body. Images are a link between intellectual and experiential processes. A link between anxiety and action. Here it would be useful to talk about archetypes. The problem so far has been that the notion of archetypes is applied to the tarot in a reductive way. Saying that LA LVNE is Jung's "male unconscious femininity" doesn't give us any real understanding of how archetypes work, because trying to fit the tarot into Jungian archetypes is merely an anecdotal exercise. The truth is that Jung barely mentioned the tarot in his writings, and when he did so he did it from the perspective of someone who had never experienced it first hand. He wasn't thinking on the specific images of the tarot when he wrote about archetypes, but he left us a very useful notion of archetypes as a structure for the unconscious mind.

When we feel the fear that cannot be named and are told we are 'depressed', we are left without means to grasp our problem. 'Depression' is an abstraction. At best we could ask *"what should I take for that?"* But if we are invited to take our nameless fear and pour it into LA LVNE, our fear materializes in the form of tides, day and night, moon cycles, and the sudden nervousness of beasts. Right then we understand that no matter how dark darkness can get, it always changes. Pain is a moment. It can always recede, even if just temporarily.

LVNE is: Soul: VE and Body: LN

The letter V always suggests the influence of heaven, and in the tarot we see how the final trumps sequence accords progressively more space to the skies. But it would be good to acknowledge that the crayfish, the two dogs, and the two towers are creating the same letter V. Nature has become receptive! The letter E here seems to articulate three levels of action: there is the moon on top, irradiating droplets, then the two dogs, sucking them, and then the crayfish, hoping to catch at least a few. We can also see the letter E in three levels of the image: a strip of heaven, a strip of earth, and a strip of sea. In any case, VE seems to invite us to think about how every event shades its influence in layers. We never really know how deeply an event is touching us, or how many levels a single event can reach.

The black L on the white background looks like a tower washed by moonlight. The letter N reminds us that there are two towers, not one, and that these two towers are separated by a distance that the diagonal line in the middle of the letter depicts as dynamic. *The bridge between towers is as long or as short as we feel it to be*. Determining the length of the bridge won't be as important as realizing the subjectivity of its measurements. This way we are told that waiting is better than giving up. If the distance seems insurmountable today, it will feel shorter tomorrow.

Each tarot image is a talisman against fear.

LE SOLEIL

On the tenth station of the cross in the church of Renne Le Chateau one can see three dice. The visible numbers on the dice's faces are: 3, 4 and 5. Since dice are also present in Le Bateleur, this has been taken as definitive proof of the connection between the tarot and the mysteries of the grail. I guess this follows the same logic as saying that our freckles are constellations mirroring the stars, and therefore, dermatologists rule the universe.

Although no one has yet mentioned the similarities between the hats of Le Bateleur's and Indiana Jones's, all kind of numerological ruses have been employed to further demonstrate how the tarot conceals the secret of the grail. Let's play with the numbers on Renne Le Chateau's dice: we are told by the experts that if we multiply 3×4 we get 12. If this isn't impressive enough, get this: If we then add 5 to 12, we get 17. I gather you aren't mesmerized yet, but wait. Card 17 in the tarot is Lestoille. See? There you have Mary Magdalene herself, doing the holy dishes!

Making connections is a form of mental gymnastics. In our game with shapes we must keep the bird out of the cage because we know that, as soon as we lock it in, it becomes a shadow of itself. Shapes have a voice, but nothing they say should be taken as the last word. If we want the game of tarot to help us grow, the act of seeing has to be more important than what we see. If making connections prove something, it is that we can make connections. Nothing more, nothing less. Even so, in the midst of such connections we can arrive at unexpected insights. Keeping that always in mind, let us continue our little game by looking at LE SOLEIL.

SOLEIL is: Soul: OEI and Body: SLL

All is clear, in broad sunlight, since both SLL and OEI seem to convey very direct messages. SLL suggests being nourished by heaven (letter S) so we can expand within the world (letter L). But we see two letters L, suggesting that we aren't supposed to do this alone. Either we see these two letters L as two different persons, as in a partnership or a couple, or we see them as two halves of ourselves: masculine and feminine, active and receptive. In both cases, our expansion in the world depends on their being united. That is what the letters OEI are talking about. In them we can see the main scene depicted in LE SOLEIL: two characters, one masculine (the letter I) and the other feminine (the letter O) extend their arms and legs (letter E) to embrace each other as one single being.

The tarot's lore tells us that in LE SOLEIL a child who can see is lending his eyes to a blind one. This is a beautiful metaphor for the kind of communion the letters OEI are suggesting. Maybe we need to borrow the eyes of another to be truly complete. Perhaps then we will realize that the only mystery to unlock by searching for hidden clues and connections in the world around us is the mystery of ourselves.

LE IVGEMENT

Soul: EIVEE Body: LGMNT.

Look at the soul: EIVEE. The first thing we notice is a horizontal motion emphasized by the presence of three letters E. Repeated in this way, these letters seem to suggest the flow of life, our minds, hearts and bodies rushing forward, sometimes without knowing were are we going or why. We live in catacombs dug out bit by bit, by walking the same paths day after day, by tasting the same flavors over and over, by listening to the same tunes once and again, without even noticing that by repeating ourselves we have turned into ghosts.

In EIVEE, the flow of life is suspended by a call from above.

The letter I reminds us to stop. Day after day we walk along with the herd, but, do we really want to go where the herd is going? When we mimic a letter with our body we understand what its shape is saying. Just as the letter I is telling us to stand still, the letter V suggests we should look up and become receptive to the sky. It opens itself to heaven: it is open to inspiration from whatever exists outside the flow of our routine. Standing as a little unit in the center of LE IVGEMENT's soul, the letter V reminds us that hope is in the details. Keep a candle by your window, so those who are lost can find their way home. Carry a deck of cards in your pocket, so you will always have the option of building a castle. Get a top hat and you will always have the possibility of pulling out a rabbit. Why? Because every time you refuse to kiss a toad you are denying a prince.

The word's body is also very eloquent: LGMNT. It starts with a letter L and ends with a letter T. In other words, the horizontal emphasis of the letter L gets redirected to a vertical emphasis in the letter T, reinforcing the idea of looking up from time to time. Both letters L and T seem to be saying: "Stop walking with your eyes. Your feet know where they need to go." In order to look up and find inspiration, the letter G suggests that we dispel any false sense of wholeness by performing an act of attention which will take us back inside ourselves. The letter G seems to be pointing its thumb towards its heart, as if to say: "Looking within is a way to be reborn over and over". Then, to avoid falling into selfishness, the letter G is followed by the letter M, which advises us to find someone else to hold hands with. Inspiration is worthless if we can't share it. But clinging to others can also prevent us from being inspired. For this reason, the letter M is followed by the letter N, which reminds us to always maintain a healthy distance, even from those who are closest to us, and that comes from independence.

In some old decks, LE IVGEMENT is renamed 'Fame'. This may be relevant, since recognition is indeed re-cognition. Something is renowned when we dare pay enough attention to know that we know it. Focusing on the routine elevates it. But, what if that humdrum routine is ourselves?

LE IVGEMENT. These ten letters are telling us that, like a bear emerging from its den after the winter, we resurrect every morning. But we need to stop and take notice if we want to really wake up.

LESTOILLE – LEMONDE

In an interview, artist Damien Hirst said "You might say very clever things just by feeling your way in the dark." I think he has a point. By feeling our way in the dark, we learn to create a whole reality based only on the few things we manage to touch. This way we learn that when an experience is presented to us we don't need to pay attention to everything. No matter how big a river may be, we only need a few sips of water to quench our thirst. The tarot's images are full of colors, details, symbols and characters. Trying to understand an image by scanning each single color, each single symbol and each single detail in it would be like gulping down the whole river! That's why we compare one image to another, one name to another, so we can pay attention only to these few things that, by being repeated more than once, are impressed upon us. We find a message in the similarities among images. Then we qualify that message by noticing the differences between these similar things.

What is in the soul of words? The vowels always carry a vibrant message. When we unlock LESTOILLE and LEMONDE to look at their souls, a similarity catches our eye. LESTOILLE's soul is EOIE, while LEMONDE's soul is EOE. This is enough for us to work on and wonder. But let us now give the consonants a rest.

EOIE–EOE

We cannot help be inspired by the fact that the souls of these two words are so similar, especially since the two images also resemble each other: both feature a blond woman as main character. This blond woman, free of clothing to represent freedom from material burdens, is often thought to be the soul, the anima, or the anima mundi. In other words, the soul of two words representing souls is almost identical, just as the women depicted in the images.

Almost.

When two things are alike, we will find more information in their differences than in their similarities.

In EOE, we see LEMONDE as ephemeral glory. The horizontal flow of the letter E contrasts with the self-centeredness of the letter O. That letter O, which reminds us of the mandorla centered on our woman, stands between the two letters E. This tells us that glory is like an Inn we find at the roadside. We can enjoy its comfort for a night or two, but then we must keep going. In any case, there is a fluid rhythm in these three letters: 'advance' (first letter E), 'rejoice' (letter O), 'advance' (second letter E), that could be translated as "rather be a river than a pond". On the other hand, EOIE shows a stop in the rhythm illustrated by the letter I, as in an errand we must run before feeling free to dance with the world.

The letter I regards the letter O like an individual staring at a void; or more precisely, like the woman in LESTOILLE who stares at the river into which she pours the contents of her jars. With the letter I beside the letter O, the woman is standing outside of the mandorla, and we notice that if the letter I jumps into the letter O, it will create the image in LE MONDE. The letters O and I are telling us that, if the woman in LESTOILLE wants to become the woman in LEMONDE, she needs to release all that water, and then throw her entire self into the stream. No river holds itself back.

It is a good thing that we have the tarot to help us reflect on such things. As in any other kind of poetry, visual poetry should help us build ourselves a soul. It is so hard to do this on our own that we can't help but envy how lucky diamonds are. Diamonds can take thousands of years to go from dust to light. We have only a few decades to attain our full lustre.

An Engine Also Known as The Jackalope Theory

TAROT* expands** SEMANTIC FIELDS***

*a tarot card's height is twice its width
so it can rest on top
of a new word
and an old word
at once

the tarot is a set of images
whose main property
is the potential to heal
language

people problems = language problems
fortunately,
images are solid
readily meltable
substances
for insertion into a linguistic cavity

**EFFECT
Lepus cornutus
can be a Jackalope
or a rabbit suffering
from Shope papillomavirus

diagnosis won't spare
the rabbit from his thorned style
but an image can be his alibi

I bet you'd rather be
a Jackalope
than 'the papilloma guy'

METHOD
a rabbit is
a rabbit
and papilloma isn't
a papillon
but when we add
rabbit + papilloma
a tumor on the head becomes
a horn

the head expands
the tumor
to include the idea of an antler
the antler expands
the rabbit
to include the idea of
a stag

(thanks to that, the poor
thing doesn't have
to wear a cap)

***a constellation
of units
of meaning
weaving in a synaptic chain
everything that exists
so a thought can never
jump
out
of
its

electric fence

Tarot's Quarantine

the tarot is ill

kidnapped, raped and brainwashed
the tarot has developed

Stockholm Syndrome

it's images have lost their memory
Memory has lost its images

doctors recommend keeping it away from people who
want fortunetelling
deaf-eyed

eager beavers
and from anybody claiming to have an open chakra

until it can be restored to a state of poetic uncertainty

it would be advisable
doctors say
for the tarot to be exposed
to the sight of image-makers
and those who know that knowledge
is useless before illusion

enshrouded in a pungent glare

the tarot must remain in quarantine
until we can grant
its freedom of silence

NOTE: *following Greyfriars Bobby's example, and as part of the tarot's quarantine, I will be conducting 303,824,640 one-on-one discussions with those interested on helping the images recover their memory.*

the quarantine will be lifted shortly after I am done

How to Turn a Deck of Cards Into a Thermometer

(learning social sculpture from a Hare)

red is warm

black is cold

1 is contracted
10 is expanded

from 1 to 2 or 3
things go slow

from 1 to 6 or 9
things go fast

pips are patterns
courts are people
pips are inner
courts are outer

all that falls between
"Once Upon a Time" and "Happily Ever After"
is about going

from warm to cold
from cold to warm

about contracting if you have expanded
about expanding if you are contracted

because you are a lump of clay

(and I mean it nicely)

Tarot Side-Effects

WARNING: extended use of the tarot can cause dependence; vision or speech changes; tightness in the chest; lightheadedness when sitting up or standing; confusion; fainting; difficult swallowing; vomit that looks like famous people; fast or pounding heartbeat; falling; fever; hallucinations; mental or mood changes; temporary impairment of the ability to make sensible judgments and understand common dangers; an impulse to wander. Don't use the tarot if you can't take responsibility for your own life, if you suffer from an extravagant or irrational devotion or if you are prone to a pathological displacement of erotic interest and satisfaction towards fortunetelling.

La Conspiration Alphabétique

(an infallible method to reveal the name of a future husband, wife, or partner)

a = Ace de Deniers
b = Le Bateleur
c = La Pances* (La Papesse)
d = Imperatris
e = Ace de Epees
f = Lempereur
g = Le Pape
h = Lamoureu
i = Le Fol
j = Le Charior
k = Iustice
l = Lermite
m = La Roue de Fortun
n = Force
o = Ace de Baton
p = Le Pandu
q = *(Arcane sans nom)*
r = Temperance
s = Le Diable
t = La Maison Dieu
u = Ace de Coupes
v = Le Toille
w = La Lune
x = Le Soleil
y = Le Judgement
z = Le Monde

method:

1.
shuffle the deck (only the trumps plus the four aces) and pull from four to eight cards.

2.
using the above table of correspondences, translate the card's sequence into letters.

3.
put all those letter together, creating a word.

4.
read the word
plan a: these random words will contain an actual name.
plan b: making anagrams of these words you will find another word whose sound, etymology or meaning will lead you to a name.

5.
look for a person with that name

6.
marry that person

example:

Le Fol (i) + Le Pandu (p) + Ace de Deniers (a) + La Rove de Fortun (m) + Lamoureu (h) = ipamh
Ipamh = **I, Pam H.**

In the above example, we are encouraged to look for a person whose first name is 'Pam', and whose last name should start withy the letter H, or sounds like *"aych"*.

We guarantee this method will lead you to absolute happiness, until the need of shuffling the deck again becomes evident. **

* In adherence to a science of the circumstantial, these card names follow the Jean Dodal spelling, because that was the deck that happened to be on the table.

** RESULTS NOT TYPICAL

DISCLAIMER: we strongly disclaim whatever you may think we are claiming.

La Conspiration Alphabétique (Appendix)

(This appendix is brought to you with limited commercial interruptions by the word 'befuddlement')

Those who already have a husband, wife, or partner (and won't surrender to the temptation of shuffling the deck again), could apply our table of correspondences to the name of a significant other. The resulting card-sequence will accurately predict an imaginary fate for that relationship. The pataphysical nature of the tarot-as-machine cannot be overlooked, for it allow us to make all kinds of predictions *as if* reality* were supposed to mirror the imaginary solutions we propose. Even so, it would be important to note that every single idea posed to us by the tarot gets automatically disclaimed by the tarot's artificial nature. The tarot is not 'reality', but an alternative to reality. It doesn't stand beyond that what is real, but aside of what is real (slightly to the right, we suspect). It will be of foremost importance to keep in mind that, by telling a future *as if,* instead of telling a future *as is*, the tarot always disclaims itself.

(befuddlement = bed-melted fun)

Translating a sequence of cards into a word may seem limited or limiting, but turning the procedure the other way around offers limitless possibilities. Any word can be translated into a sequence of cards, and therefore, any word can be expanded into many other words. If we understand poetry as the realm where language is re-created, we will see the tarot as the ultimate poetical machine, for it allows us to operate outside the frontier of language by decomposing words into images, so the semantic field of our original words get expanded by absorbing the semantic fields of all the words included in these images, once we translate the images back to language. As Italo Calvino rightly wrote: "the most artificial of mechanisms is capable of awakening in us the most secret and unexpected poetic demons".

For example, the proposed methodology would expand the word LOVE into this card sequence:

(L) Lermite + (O) Ace de Batons + (V) La Maison Dieu + (E) Ace de Spees = A lonely man, stuck in the memory of his past, is offered a blazing branch that destroys his rational boundaries, giving him a new will to live.

(befuddlement = feet blend mud)

A tarologist searches for that anomaly where chaos makes perfect sense. The aim of our mechanistic methodologies would be to provide viable alternatives to what Mallarmé called "spiritual anarchy" and we know as 'inspiration'. By denying inspiration – illustrated in this case as the serendipitous calling of Love – and by substituting it by a whole new set of constraints, we hope to arrive at the same results chance would produce – in this case, a "happy ever after" marriage – by feasible means. Even so, it must be clear that finding love is just a secondary application for this poetic device.

(This appendix was brought to you with limited commercial interruptions by the word 'befuddlement'. Let us know if these commercials were useful to you)

* In order to get the most accurate perspective, it would be useful to understand reality as "everything else but me". This makes more likely for the tarot-as-a-dream to overlap reality-as-a-dream.

PATAPHYSICAL POETRY

A Pragmatic Paradigm of Pataphysical Para-grammaticism

(**WARNING**: *all the letters C in the following text have been flipped 180 degrees over their horizontal axis. Viewer discretion is advised*)

The following procedure hopes to turn our eyes into a cat who brings live prey to its owner. Here, we will be unveiling the hidden semantic value that lies within words. Once again we will use the tarot – more precisely, the tarot card's names – as a generator of random input. As a prosthetic unconscious, and even inside its box, we can trust that the tarot's images exist in a random alignment which is pre-verbal, arbitrary, non-intentional, and potentially meaningful: a swerve ready to swerve*. Those of you who think that words simply stand for their linguistic value will soon discover a way of getting more bang for your buck; but before attempting this technique we recommend you master the Chinese Linking Rings illusion. This way you will learn that what is linked can be broken, and what is detached can be linked, since the difference between a link and a gap is just a matter of semantics.

The method we propose is extremely simple:

Take three random cards and place them in a horizontal row. Write down the name of these three cards separating them by commas.

Example:

le charior, le soleil, le toille

Now, look for another word/words hiding in plain sight within that word.

Example:

plucked

  luck

Once we *see* that the word 'plucked' contains the word 'luck', a sense of joy only comparable to the exhilaration of figuring out how to turn a studio apartment into a two bedrooms will overcome us. Words will no longer have the same simplicity. Right then and there, a whole new level of meaning opens to us in an instance of deviant linguistic behavior, leaving insight in sight. (This procedure, which we already demonstrated in our *ars tarotica*, has been eloquently exploited by Canadian poet bp Nichol, whose Martyrology series we wholeheartedly recommend, even if you have no interest in our shenanigans).

We will focus here on how this method can be used to get all kinds of very specific, imaginary, answers.

Example:

are we looking for the name of a future boyfriend?

le charior, le soleil, le toille

   char   le s

what will be his most attractive feature?

le charior, le soleil, le toille

   h i   s

   ha i r

are we looking for a girlfriend?

le charior, le soleil, le toille

   har r   i et e

where would we meet her?

le charior, le soleil, le toille

   a

   h   il l

what will be her favorite food?

le charior, le soleil, le toille

    e   e l

      r o l   l

would these cards give us any final message?

le charior, le soleil, le toille

    a

h or s e

   i   s

          to

   a

cha i r

   a   s

   a

c ar

   i   s

        to

   a

h or s e

```
                or

                        so

    e ch    o

        ha      s

            i           t
```

The natural order of things implies that our questions could be given imaginary answers by the words we find within words. We can also turn the procedure around and let the answers provided by these words within words dictate imaginary questions to us.

Example:

lemonde, lermite, le bateleur

```
                            a

    mo          te  l

                    ba      r
```

question: where should I go?

lemonde, lermite, le bateleur

```
                        a

    l           ite
```

lemon

                          b ee r

question: what should I drink?

lemonde, lermite, le bateleur

    on e

 m   i le

question: how far is that bar from home?

lemonde, lermite, le bateleur

               a

le   t   te r

question: what would I find there?

While this procedure may not appease our current conundrums, it may suggest an imaginary alternative to our immediate reality, and therefore, a viable course of action. That is, after all, all we need when we feel stuck. When random answers suggest random questions they regale us with imaginary problems, and we are left with the script for a performance piece we could put into action at any time our actual situation becomes unbearable. After all, few things feel better than going to a bar a mile away from home, have a lite lemon beer and look for letter-shapes in the stains of the bar's countertop.

The versatility of this device gets confirmed by the fact that we can have a question answering itself, in the event of the tarot's unexpected absence.

Example:

would the magician make a good husband?

```
                a

            n   ake    d

        m   i   m  e

    h   a              s

        a

                       s a d

w       a   n      d
```

(NOTE: That was an actual question posed at a rather popular on-line tarot forum. We never use professional drivers nor closed courses in our demonstrations)

It should be obvious by now that the same method can be applied to the names of people (or pets, for goodness' sake!), titles, systematic classifications or random phrases. Although our aim is to simply soothe an itch (there must be better things to do with language than speak it!) it seems crucial for us, tarologists, to bring forward the oracular value in language. After all, we read for, or on behalf of, an audience of non-readers. Such a non-reader is mainly interested in a word's magical efficacy, not in its aesthetic impact**.

This magical pursuit, which is nothing more than a guileless attempt at using poetry to affect our surroundings rather than ourselves, manifests, in the non-reader's view, as the sudden emergence of meaning which inhabits the tension between the original word and the ones we uncover. Our perception of a word is modified by its internal organs – its vowels as viscera – therefore affecting the non-reader at a gut level. Just as each tarot card in a sequence swerves the meaning of the previous one (compare for a moment how the meaning of Le Fol is affected when followed by La Maison Dieu or when followed by Le Soleil) a word's meaning is swerved by any word it contains. For example, in a proposition like:

husband

s and

'Husband' not only turns into 'sand' is terms of spelling. The fact that 'husband' becomes 'sand' is in itself the meaning of our little operation, or so we pataphysically assume. 'Sand' turns 'husband' into the narrative of its own predicaments. As poet Bruce Andrews wrote: "Meaning is not produced by the sign, but by the contexts we bring to the potentials of language".

When it comes to facing forms, meaning is all we have. Although the poetic use of aleatory devices always involves the lascivious interaction of chance and choice***, we trust that paranoia creates the memory of its own birth. We guarantee that if you use the above method you will end up standing at approximately two degrees from the truth.

* A 'swerve' has been defined as a "sudden deviation". When we say that each tarot card swerves the previous one we mean that our perception of a tarot card's meaning gets altered/deviated by the following card. Moreover, the word swerve contains both the words 'we' and 'serve', confirming the tarot images's readiness to generate meaning if we are as fools as those who were petrified by Medusa, and look at them.

** Is this 'magical efficacy' really different from aesthetic impact? We doubt it. In fact, we conceive any divinatory use we make of the tarot as a covert poetic act. (We hope Dick Higgins would agree).

*** Chance stepped out of the shower. A grin spread over her face, as Choice's hands closed over her arms. Choice pulled Chance's gently but forcefully into his arms, Choice's hands disposing of Chance's towel and moving to Chance's ass, pulling Chance's hips hard into Choice's. Chance's breasts were crushed against Choice's chest, and Choice's lips came to devour Chance's, Choice's tongue plunging into Chance's mouth.

Predicting the Present

(On the Impropriety of Looking at Tarot Cards Over a Horizontal Plane)

"I have never experienced intellectual pleasure except on the analogical level. For me, what is unmistakably *real* is determined by the spontaneous, clairvoyant, insolent relation that, under certain conditions, connects one thing with another." André Bretón

1.

It can be argued that, quite often, water has an elongated, cylindrical shape, resembling pipes and hoses. This gets confirmed by the fact that, if we were to slice a pipe, we will see how each slice has the shape of a letter O, and the letter O is analogous to a drop of water. (See Fig. 1.)*

Fig. 1.

O = O

⠀⠀⠀O

⠀⠀⠀O

⠀⠀⠀O

⠀⠀⠀O

○
○
○
○
○
○

2.

The tarot's hypertrophied biography should be contested by the tarot's own barefaced slapstick, so these cards can regain their status as what Alfred Jarry called a "hypothetical novel". Mining the tarot for coincidences should have us reaching that moment of accurate enactment that can make the unreal real and the real unreal. We must, then, place the tarot images in the proper context: 'here', in our 'reality'. How do we accomplish that? We could start by defining 'here' as "except everywhere else" and 'reality' as "everything else but me", (therefore I am Here, or, I = Here). In order to determine its representational value with uttermost exactitude, each tarot card should be held at arm's length, turning its negligible homunculi into life-sized characters**.

Held at that distance, we see how the tarot is as ridiculous as reality, and therefore perfectly able to both represent and substitute it. Moreover, overlapping reality brings forward the tarot's instantaneous illuminative power (See Fig. 2.).

Fig 2.

HALLUCINATION = A LUCID NATION

3.

What such conjunction accomplishes is the creation of a moment of beauty which is expressed as an Aha! Moment of analogical proportions. Beauty is the ultimate time machine, in that, as Breton claimed, it has the ability to stop time. We are only truly 'here' when we experience beauty, which means that beauty is that time machine that can finally take us to the present, away from our memories of the past and away from our anxiety of the future. (This would explain why eclipses are one of the very few moments in which we truly live in the present).

It is, thus, by these procedures that the tarot can predict the present, which is the most elusive state known to men.

It should be noticed here that the present predicted by the tarot is not a representation of whatever we think our current situation is, for the tarot doesn't represents what *it is*, but creates *as if it is*. After all, the tarot's main function is to re-create language. In turn, language's main function is to create reality. (Which is why the best way to boil an egg is to write the words **'HOT WATER'** on its shell, and the best way to glue two objects together is to write the word **'AND'** between them). We cannot emphasize enough the imaginary nature of any present predicted by the tarot, for it is precisely this imaginary quality what makes it viable. In other words, if reality *as it is* couldn't be surpassed nor improved by our imagination, we wouldn't need the tarot at all.

4.

To understand the tarot is to understand the art and science of surviving our own death, which is akin to accepting that we can only under-stand the act of dying.

* Fig. 1. Shouldn't be confused with Fig. 3., a popular item in most S&M shops.

Fig. 3.

O-O-O-O-O-O-O-O

** **We are told that our friend, master card-maker Jean-Claude Flornoy, has made himself a life-size tarot deck. He may have short arms, but he certainly has ginormous pockets.**

NOTICE: The inner curvature of the letter O is strictly confidential and reserved solely to the addressees. If received by persons differing from the addressee, the inner curvature of the letter O may not be divulged, distributed or copied in any way. If you have seen the inner curvature of the letter O by mistake, please inform us and destroy and/or delete it from your computer. This message (including any annexes) shall not be considered an alphabetic proposal and/or acceptance of phonemes from the addressee, or a waiver or acknowledgement of formal objects and/or open syllables; neither shall it be binding when not followed by a subsequent utterance signed by subjects able to lawfully represent us. We decline all pre-alphabetic liability when the letter O is not followed by any utterance signed by the parties.

Letters are Figures of Speech

"I heard a voice say from afar that the incomprehensible is solely the result of incomprehension, which seeks what is has and therefore can never make further discoveries". Novalis

Part of a private club that welcomes no non-members, known as 'the alphabet'. One day we will direct your attention to how the letter **N** shows the perfect way of vanishing an elephant: when the elephant enters the letter **N** (See fig. 1.) one only has to hide it behind the large mirror that runs diagonally between the letter **N**'s parallel walls. Once the elephant is in place, the letter **N** is rotated 180 degrees clock-wise. The audience will think they are seeing an empty letter **N**, when in truth they are looking at one half of the interior, and its reflection. (This illusion is so effective that we are inclined to suspect all letters **N** conceal an elephant inside of them at all times).

Fig 1.

Ñ

But we don't want to distract you. Please focus now on the only image in the Marseille tarot that has no number (**F**) and on the only image that bears no name (**L**). While the letter **F** projects itself forward, from the waist up, running the risk of being brought down in its pursuit by its own lack of foundation, the letter **L** levels the field, untouched by any longing. The letter **L** is devoid of a future just as the black soil is the void of the present.

151

It is for this reason that the Marseille tarot's folklore has both images overlapping. (See Fig. 2.)

Fig 2.

F + L = E

Similar analogical conclusions can be reached after studying a few other basic tarological operations (See Fig. 3.)

Fig 3.

U – I = J

I + V = N

V + V = W

I – I = H

I + X = K

I + D = P

I + V = Y

I + V + I = M

(We will be particularly delighted if you noticed how the two horses in the letter **H** are the same human-like creatures at once chained and pulled apart that we see in the letter **M**).

152

Still, the practical nature of these images won't be totally clear until we understand that Lempereur is the fourth trump, it bears the Roman numeral **IIII** written at the top, and it shows an old man looking at a number 4 carved on 'midair', right in front of him, whose posture he imitates by crossing his legs* in a similar fashion. With his gesture Lempereur is teaching us how to use the Marseilles tarot. He invites us to "follow the sign", silently hinting at the analogical nature of the tarot's message.

We are finite, both in imagination and experience. (There are questions we ask ourselves for years before finding an answer to them, for instance, if a narrative of clouds would cluster in a coherent syntax, and if we could replicate it by blowing up smoke). Using the tarot doesn't consist of describing a person's life by resorting to a fixed repertoire of images, but of describing an image by using our fixed repertoire of life experiences. Not only is human experience defined by a limited range of possibilities, but the access each one of us has to these possibilities has been restricted by the attributes of our personality. The easier it is to imitate an image, the easier it is for us to comprehend it. (See Fig. 4.).

Fig. 4.

O = yawn*

* Remember: while the letter **d** sits on its throne, looking at the past with its legs crossed, the letter **p** mirrors this posture from an upside-down position, its hair always about to tickle the ground. (See Fig. 5.)

Fig 5.

d = p

** Yes, yes... yawning at this point would confirm that you have understood how the Marseilles tarot operates.

DISCLAIMER: No yawn is authorized to elicit any yawning on behalf of the yawner without express confirmation by the letter O.

An Infallible Method to Foretell the Time of Imaginary Events

(on the autistic merits of tarological chronograms)

LE FOL = **LL** = 100 (100 = C)

LE BATELEVR = **LLV** = 105 (105 = CV)

LA PANCES = **LC** = 150 (50 = L)

IMPERATRIS = **IMI** = 1002 (1000 = M)

LEMPEREVR = **LMV** = 1055 (955 = CMLV)

LE PAPE = **L** = 50

LA MOVREV = **LMVV** = 1060 (960 = CMLX)

LE CHARIOR = **LCI** = 151 (51 = LI)

IVSTICE = **IVIC** = 105 (103 = CIII)

LERMITE = **LMI** = 1051 (951 = CMLI)

LA ROVE DE FORTVN = **LVDV** = 560 (550 = DL)

FORCE = **C** = 100

LE PANDV = **LDV** = 555 (455 = CDLV)

TEMPERANCE = **MC** = 1100

LE DIABLE = **LDIL** = 601 (499 = CDXCIX)

LA MAISON DIEV = **LMIDIV** = 1555 (1453 = MCDLIII)

LE TOILLE = **LILL** = 151 (149 = CXLIX)

LA LUNE = **LL** = 100 (100 = C)

LE SOLEIL = **LLIL** = 151 (149 = CXLIX)

LE IVGEMENT = **LIVM** = 1054 (1054 – MLIV)

LE MONDE = **LMD** = 1550 (1450 = MCDL)

1.

shuffle de tarot trumps. Pick only one random card.

2.

look for any of the following letters in that trump's name: **C, D, I, L, V, M, X** (Those letters stand for all known Roman numerals).

NOTE: Here we are following the spelling proposed by Jean Dodal. Any calculation based on Jean Noblet's spelling carries a two-minute delay.

3.

put them together

example:

LA MAISON DIEV = **LMIDIV**

4.

convert that figure from Roman numerals into Arabic numerals.

example:

LMIDIV = 1555

NOTE: The tarot uses an additive system for its Roman numerals. (The number 4 would be expressed as IIII instead of IV, for example). For this reason, we made all conversions by simply adding up the values corresponding to the Roman numerals hiding in the trump's names. For the sake of accuracy we have also included, in parantheses, a more correct conversion system, along with the corrected Roman cyphers. Although this might seem more truthful, we fear that any calculation you base on this system will lead to a life marked by countless disencounters and disappointments.

5.

count two numbers from right to left, and place a colon there

example:

1555 = 15:55

in the above example, La Maison Diev is encouraging us to wait until **3:55** for the imaginary event to happen.

6.

wait

WARNING: Although the exactitude of this methodology is unquestionable, we can't guarantee that the imaginary event happening at the specified time would be the one you imagined.

Our aim is to encourage you to use your imagination. In no event will we be liable for what you imagine.

NOTE ON THE USE OF IMAGINARY SOLUTIONS: The imaginary solutions contained in the tarot intend to give you the means for sabotaging reality through poetic action only. An imaginary solution should lead to practical action. An imaginary solution is not an intellectual construct, nor does it suggest a conceptual, psychlogical or spiritual inquiry. The imaginary solutions are provided by the tarologist and while he endeavours to keep the imaginary solutions 200% accurate, meaning, that any imaginary solution is twice as accurate as any other solution you haven't thought of yet, we make no representations or warranties of any kind, express or implied, about the completeness, reliability, suitability or availability of your ability to live up to your own imagination.

The tarot is a source of mechanistic insight, and therefore it is at odds with intuition. (The tarot intends to replace intuition, not to enhance it). Any reliance you place on such imaginary solutions for reasons other than poetical is therefore strictly at your own risk.

In no event will the tarologist be liable for any loss or damage whatsoever arising from the assumption that the tarot shows reality as it is, or as it will be. It is only when we preface our queries with WHAT IF that the tarot reaches its full imaginary potential. In no event will we be liable for any quandary or dilemma arising from a misunderstanding of the imaginary solutions originated by or in connection with, the use of the tarot.

Every effort is made to keep your life up and running smoothly. However, we take no responsibility for, and will not be liable for, your life being temporarily derailed due to any silly or high-spirited behavior beyond our control.

The tarot is a source of potential prototypes for potential realities, and those are not under the control of the tarologist. We have no control over the hypotheses we bring forward nor over these hypotheses that are yet to occur to us. The description of any image does not necessarily imply a recommendation or endorsing the views expressed by it. Dangerous ideas can be contained in some images. The recipient should check these images and any words attached to them for the presence of dangerous ideas. We accept no liability for any damage caused by any dangerous idea transmitted by these images.

Any sufficiently imaginative solution is indistinguishable from science.

NOTE ON THE NOTE ON THE USE OF IMAGINARY SOLUTIONS: The alphabet is nothing more, and nothing less, than the cogs and wheels of the mind-as-machine, whose blueprints we read in the form of words, and then we test in a series of prototypes we call 'reality'. As prototype, reality is just one possibility among the many others we haven't thought of yet. The attention we pay to the words we chose makes us unaware of all the other words we didn't choose. But like the owl-infected woods trapped between the parenthesis of our dreams, these other words don't go away. The words we didn't choose lurk in the space between the words we did choose. One must then realize that all these other words can also become possibilities whose viability can be tested as a reality-prototype. Here is where the Marseille tarot as a machine for imaginary solutions becomes useful, for the Marseille tarot is an imagistic abacus, doing the math of what could be. The tarot is, thus, a rich source of plan Bs.

A Cutting-Edge Extension To Our Infallible Method to Foretell the Time of Imaginary Events

"Interpretative delirium begins only when man, ill prepared,

Is taken by a sudden fear in the forest of symbols".

André Bretón

The fluctuations in hair-length* among the characters in any given sequence of cards will give us a measure of the passing of time. (If you have any doubt about the efficacy of hair at giving us an account of time passing, you just have to look at an old picture of yours and see how clearly your hair tells you how much time has passed THROUGH you). Our hair is an hourglass.

The tarot (here we actually mean the Marseille ((actually, we really mean either the Jean Noblet or the Jean Dodal tarot (((to be candid, we are partial to the Jean Dodal ((((but it has to be the Jean Dodal restored (((((ideally, the hand-stenciled edition ((((((from the copies we own, we rather like the one numbered 00241 (((((((Who are we kidding? We also like to work with the mass-printed edition ((((((((In all fairness, we are emotionally involved in the mass-printed edition (((((((((Still, considering how many people never experienced the tarot before ((((((((((They dont't know that the tarot delivers imaginary solutions to the problem of our lives)))))))))) it feels criminal to deprive them from experiencing the hand-stenciled edition))))))))) because we wrote the prologue for it)))))))) which gives us the possibility of looking at the pips))))))) than the other ones)))))) whose colors are purer))))) by master cardmaker Jean-Claude Flornoy)))) because some bits of tarot de Marseille lore that aren't present in the Noblet can be seen in the Dodal, like the blind boy in Le Soleil, Lermite's missing little finger, or the famous black bird in Le Toille))) which are the earlier ones)) tarot) is not oblivious to the wisdom of the wig**. In fact, most of the characters we see in the cards show abundant yellow hair, yellow being in itself an allusion to the time of the harvest. By choosing this color, master cardmakers Noblet, Dodal, et all, hinted at one fundamental principle in the relationship between man and Nature: when things grow, we cut them. We cannot bear the sight of something sticking out or sprouting, for we grab our scythes or scissors and chop it off.

There is infinite analogical*** wisdom to be extracted from the fact that we all have experienced the need of going to the barber, or the hairdresser (we emphatically reject using the term 'stylist' in reference to anybody lacking a proper PhD in Aesthetics). Moreover, the fact that La Lune (Arcane 18) is the only card in which we find no depiction of human hair, is very telling. Is it not the case that women cut their hair according to the moon's phases? Putting together these little pieces of symbolic information can be very useful when it comes to foretelling the happenstance of imaginary events.

For tarological purposes we will apply the following rule of thumb:

1.

Going from hairless to hairy would suggest an imaginary event happening towards the end of this month. (Or after your hair grows)

2.

Going from hairy to hairless would suggest an imaginary event happening towards the beginning of next month. (Or after you cut your hair).

3.

When no noticeable change is perceived, as in going from hairy to hairy or from hairless to hairless, we would assume that the imaginary event is imminent. (For tarological purposes, 'imminent' will be defined as "any time between now and two weeks").

(**NOTE:** These rules only apply when our client is as hirsute as the characters depicted in the cards. If the client where to be hairless and his cards hairy, or vice versa, an additional month should be added to our forecasting).

Additionally, in order to foretell the quantitative aspects of time, we can also apply the following two additional clauses:

4.

Going from hairless to hairy would suggest things are, literary, getting 'hairy'. This is a bad omen.

5.

Going from hairy to hairless would suggest things 'cleaning up'. This is a good omen.

Those who entertain doubts about the efficacy of these rules please be reassured: this is a scientific method. (If by scientific we define a method that can be proven wrong, except in the majority of cases).

* Here we also include beards, or going from beardless to bearded, and vice versa.

** We emphatically deny the fact that a certain secret society known – or not known – as *la confrérie de la perruque* ever existed, or that it was responsible for spreading the rumor about Jean-Baptiste Alliette, Etteilla, being a hairdresser. We also deny denying this.

*** Envision a bird, perched on the branch of a tree. (You could envision a bird perched on the branch of a three, but that will make it harder for you to get the idea. Still, you are free to envision whatever you want. By no means would we want to impose our mirages in your desert, or our desert in your mirage). Suddenly, the bird jumps onto another branch, and then onto another one. After a few minutes the bird has linked several branches which, as we would discover if we were to zoom-out of this imaginary scene, (and again, you are welcome to zoom-in instead, right to the point where you see a flea jumping from one of the bird's feather onto the next one, but soon enough – zoom enough? – you will find that this is a dead-end), belong to several different trees. From the bird's point of view, that succession of branches is part of the same sequence of jumps. In truth, the bird may be linking a sequoia to an elm, and then that elm to a palm tree. For the bird, its path makes perfect sense, even if for the ever jealous botanist these three trees can't be found in the same landscape.

That is the basis of analogical thinking: it has our mind jumping from one notion to the next likely one, just like a bird jumps from the branch of a sequoia to the branch of an elm, linking both trees in a meaningful pattern without any regard for their fundamental differences.

The space between two trees is virtually identical, it is just as green. The space between two letters is virtually identical. It is just as white. The space between two tarot cards is virtually identical. It is just as invisible. That is why we can find symmetry between The Hermit's back and the letter P's profile. Aren't they both hunchbacks, after all?

There are letters that mirror the blade of a sword, either in lightness, gleam or sharpness; although we won't recommend for you to test our hypothesis on your own flesh. (The inner corners of the letter K are especially hard to clean, and those wounded by them run the risk of contracting tetanus. Something similar happens with the inner angles of the W – the best representation of the Two of Cups on this side of the river –

which people tend to neglect and we often find filled with old Coke cans).

Sometimes it is hard to tell if the bird jumps because there is a branch, or if it is the bird's desire to jump what produces the branch. Either way, a bird can always resort to flying, but the human mind doesn't find comfort in the empty air. Thought feels safe traveling in patterns. Perhaps human thought isn't like a bird after all, but it resembles a camel, or one of those squirrels who glide, with their armpits flat, faking wings.

The flying squirrel needs a branch to avoid

The   void

That very same emptiness our brain resists,

for it can only remain senseless one blink at a time. To avoid the fall, a flying squirrel will jump from a tree onto a lamppost, and from the lamppost onto a letter I, proven (and proving) that such vowel is close enough. (The best method to catch a squirrel is to make the letter I spin one full turn, clockwise, so it becomes a letter O, trapping the squirrel inside).

In fact, we bet that a flying squirrel would jump from Le Bateleur to the letter A, as long as both of them stand still with their legs spread open. Out of necessity, the squirrel will even take that coin Le Bateleur is holding for an acorn, a nut, no matter if it is truly a sponge ball. A squirrel who feads on sponge balls will look like a letter Q.

Since our squirrel in now trapped (unless of course it makes a letter C by eating out a section of the letter O) we shall return to the analogy of the bird. Envision a bird going back and forth between two branches: one of them shaped as a letter Q and the other one shaped as a squirrel who grew fat from eating sponge balls. Although both shapes may present differences, the bird's feet have only four fingers with four cute hair-like claws, and therefore, a limited grasp. If it wants to perch itself, the bird must then find the similarities – forms of homologous contours its feet can hold onto – between these two branches. Above all, the bird must see such disparate things as similar. Otherwise jumping won't be possible.

Having the void as an alternative has us devoid of an alternative. We all cling to what we can grasp. Still, a warning is in order: the fact that we can map an analogy doesn't mean the analogy is 'true'. Squirrels who eat sponge balls die farting asterisks. An analogy only provides an imaginary route where there may be none. A dog might take a letter f for a hydrant. It might even pee on it and feel relieved, but we cannot expect to put off a fire by plugging a hose into a letter f. At best we will get an asthmatic sound: fffffffffffffffffffffffffffffffff... but no water. The tarologist should be as forthright about this as possible (See our note below).

There is a reason why you never wonder where letters go when you aren't using them: our inflatable alphabet plays big but packs small. For the tarologist, seeing the story in the letter is more instructive than seeing the story in the trump, for trumps advance the mnemonics of the physical body, whose understanding has little merits, while letters suggest language as an available body (or bodies) hiding in plain sight. We have been trained to see things as they are, not as what they look like. But the tarologist must drink from the letter B's nipples and prime his brain to rejoice at the infinite ways in which the letter a, in lower case, resembles a mermaid.

NOTE: The tarologist should present a disclaimer to the public. Such disclaimer will not take the form of words, but it will be expressed through a pair of clown shoes he will discretely wear while handling the tarot.

A Case Where Irrefutable Proof of the Pataphysical Nature of the Marseille Tarot is Given, Hoping to Settle the Matter Once and for All

d o c t o r f a u s t r o l l

t a r o t f o c u s d r o l l

NOTE: The above document should produce in us a true 'Ah!' moment (defined as the first half of an 'Aha!' moment, that is, the inspiring part that excludes the bureaucratic put into practice of an idea*), for it will reveal the actual purpose of the Marseille tarot: to oppose an absurd gesture to the problems of our life, so the future gets defined as the punch-line of the present.

ARGUMENTS

A Rather Compelling Allegation in Favor of Using the Marseille Tarot to Predict the 'Future

Predicting the 'future is a procedure that involves inserting an artificial narrative – such as the ones provided by the tarot de Marseille – in a person's ear, in order to replace a dated narrative after its meaning has been eroded. This prosthetic device is designed to maintain real-time motion in the realm of reality.

The 'future is a prosthetic device designed to maintain a person's sense of purpose along his/her daily motions. It should be noticed, though, that the 'future is not the future. While all these people who consult the tarot are manically concerned with their future, the tarologist only addresses the 'future (insisting on the pataphysical apostrophe before the word); that pataphysical instance where the present quotes itself as we travel through time at the speed of reality. The reason for this should be obvious: our desire to know the future gives away our ignorance of the present. The only way of not knowing what is going to happen is by turning a blind eye to what we are doing now. The consequences of such negligence can be appreciated in Fig. 1.

Fig. 1.

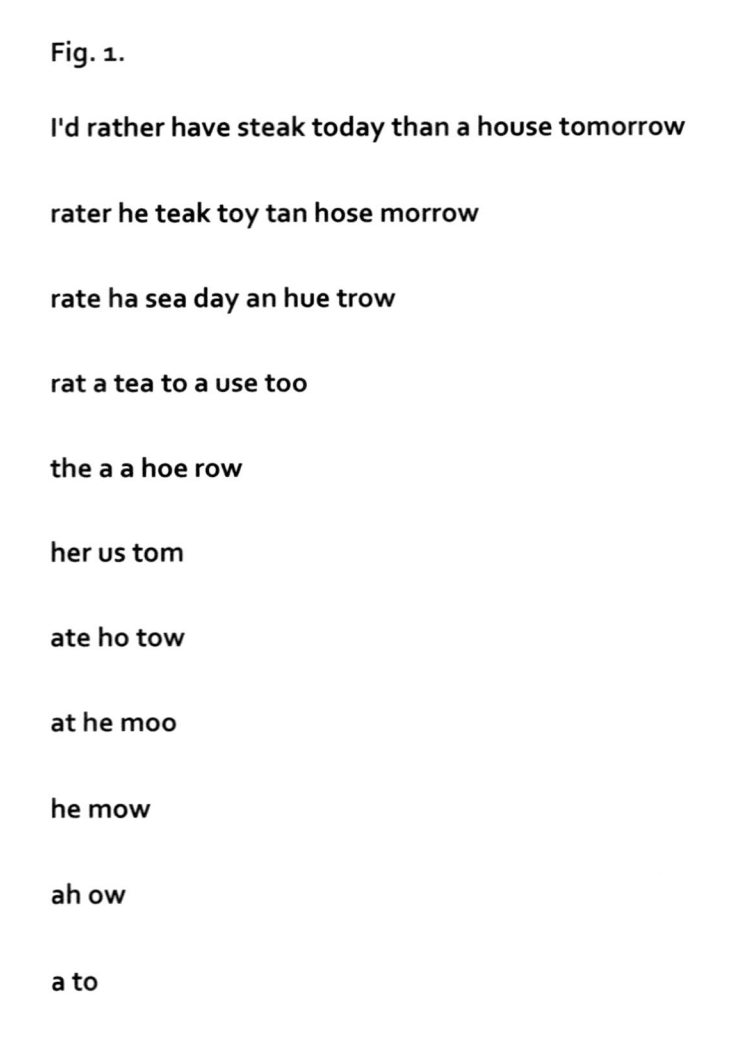

I'd rather have steak today than a house tomorrow

rater he teak toy tan hose morrow

rate ha sea day an hue trow

rat a tea to a use too

the a a hoe row

her us tom

ate ho tow

at he moo

he mow

ah ow

a to

Most people exist in a state of total ignorance of the present. But there is no reason to worry. For those who don't know that a broken window is simply the other half of a thrown stone, a 'future can be told in which the present is recounted.

(Either 'future or 'future' are pretty ambiguous statements, just as all the other words in the dictionary are ambiguous statements; words like 'mother' or 'house', which mean nothing while they travel through air, and everything when they tickle our ears*. The tarologist may, or may not, make a point to disclaim all these differences. If he chooses to do so, he will manage to enclose such disclaimer in a smile. So, be warned: whenever the tarologist smiles, he is disclaiming what he has just told you).

What attracts the tarologist to the tarot in the first place is the absurdity of seeing grown up people looking at little images in the hope of facing real-life problems by pondering imaginary solutions. (The tarologist favors that route because he knows that only madmen would do the opposite, and counter an imaginary treat with a real solution). This deliciously bizarre phenomena has its basis in the fact that human beings are capable of manufacturing material objects. Human beings also have the ability to allow these material objects to have an emotional effect on them. The vernacular term for such uncanny phenomena is 'art'. For the tarologist, the Marseille tarot allows for a prosthetic madness, necessary in order to prevent reality from achieving its ultimate goal: to drive us crazy.

The 'future is an imaginary solution that essentially functions like a joint, allowing for flexion, extension, side bending and rotating between yourself and the present.

Narratives are very important for the normal mobility and function of your body in space. When healthy, they act as "scripts" so the brain can activate the individual systems of the body within a perceived sense of meaning. Over time, narratives can become dried out, compressed or otherwise damaged, due to contradicting experiences, disappointment, and everyday wear-and-tear. When this happens, the body may loose its sense of purpose, therefore impairing its ability to move through space in a confident manner. The loss of a sense of purpose may result in pain, numbness, weakness, muscle spasms and loss of coordination, both at a personal and a professional level. (Similar symptoms, however, may occur if the person is lazy, or due to the effects of booze, or because of the common cold).

When the stories you tell about yourself fail to give you a sense of direction, the tarologist may predict a 'future for you. The 'future is the panacea of the present. The goal of predicting the 'future is to remove all or part of a damaged narrative, relieve peer-pressure and to restore a sense of possibility after your faith on the old narrative has expired.

It is easy to predict the 'future: it will be everything else except for what won't happen; just as the past is everything else but what didn't happen and the present is everything else but what isn't happening. At a microscopic level, the tarologist knows that every word he says predicts the following one (it is easy to predict the next word in a sentence: it will be any word in the dictionary, except for all the other ones we won't choose). At a macroscopic level, instead of predicting what you will be doing at any given time in the 'future, the tarologist will predict what he will be predicting for you at any given time in the 'future. That way, no matter at which point of the 'future you may be, there will always be a prediction waiting to be predicted for you. From this point of view, the 'future is always orange, and it is always dangling at the end of a stick.**

To predict the 'future, the tarologist will place each single rolled word over the tip of his tongue, whilst pinching the tip of the word enough to leave a half inch space of wiggle-room. The tarologist will then roll the word all the way down to the base of his tongue, and smooth out any air bubbles. (Air bubbles can cause a word to break, therefore altering its meaning, and the whole 'future altogether. See **Fig. 2.**).

Fig. 2.

B R E A K

B   E A K

B   E   A   K

The tarologist will insert these smooth-out words in your auditive cavity, one at a time. Sometimes the tarologist may reinsert a word several times if he considers its meaning to be of fundamental importance, or if he suspects you are missing the point.

If some extra lubrication is needed, the tarologist will put it on the first letter of the word, using always a sugar-based lubricant with harsh words, as a sour-based lubricant will cause your ears to shut down.

As with any game of chance, predicting the 'future with the tarot de Marseille is not without risk. There is the risk that this 'future will never happen, and may not relieve you, or it may worsen your original problems. It is for this reason that the tarologist always has a second opinion, or a third, or a fourth one, ready.

* It would be important to ponder the relationship between the volume in which a word is uttered and the measurements of the auricular cavity receiving that word. All letters share the same height (except for those which exhibit flexible appendixes, easy to inhale and to swallow, like the h, p, b, d, q, etcetera), which guarantees they won't scar the palate of those who pronounce them. But the fact that a scream demands a wider opening of the mouth suggests the height of screamed words to be bigger than the height of whispered words. While the oral cavity can be adjusted to several different word heights, the auricular cavity only comes in a standard measure (its size is equivalent to the little finger, as it is shown in L'Ermite). This would imply that a screamed word would tear our ears. The pain inflicted by such tearing would affect the word's meaning, potentially making it into the worst meaning of the word.

** Although this may seem a description of a wooden-legged lady showing-off her Crocs®, we are in fact talking about a carrot.

An Argument On the Benefits Of Looking At The Face Of Beauty And Not At The Rear End Of Knowledge

L A L A N G U E D E S O I S E A U X

A N A L O G U E S E X U A L I S E D

NOTE:
Since chance is irrefutable,
anagrams are the ultimate form of truth.

La langue des oiseaux turns *occultists* into *oculists*.

13 Arguments On The Polisemantic Value Of The Tarot Trumps

    O seed

            Q sprout

    O eye

            Q magnifying glass

    O beardless face

            Q bearded face

    O wall mirror

            Q hand-held mirror

    O cloud

            Q lightning

    O beach ball

            Q blue balloon

    O frog's egg

Q tadpole

O moon

Q comet

O le monde

Q le diable

O toe

Q nail

O glass

Q mug

O hungry mouth

Q chicken leg

O turtle

Q showing it's tail

A LITTLE SAMPLER OF TAROLOGICAL DEVICES (I)

metaphor

(le fol + ace de deniers) she will go places in life

(valet de baston + le pandv) I am going to give him a boost

(chevalier de épée + la maison diev) I demolished his argument

(ace de denier = ace de covpe) he is on top of it

(VIIII de baston + lermite) he can't see what is ahead

(IIII de denier + VIII de denier) my income doubled this year

(arcane VIII + valet de covpe) she will wipe you out

(reine de denier + la rove de fortvn) you are wasting your time

(V de baston + VII de baston + VIIII de baston) the opposition grows stronger

(VIIII de baston + le fov + VI de baston) he is not out of the woods yet

metonymy

a crown stands for a head

a sword stands for a battle

a coin stands for a fortune

a cup stands for a party

a branch stands for the woods

a couple stands for humanity

pun

le fol can't hang up his spoon

repetition

the II de épée has a flower at its center

the III de épée has a red sword at its center

the IIII de épée has a flower at its center

the V de épée has a red sword at its center

the VI de épée has a flower at its center

the VII de épée has a red sword at its center

the VIII de épée has a flower at its center

the VIIII de épée has a red sword at its center

where the II de baston shows two wild flowers

the III de baston shows a tamed pole

where the IIII de baston shows two wild flowers

the V de baston shows a tamed pole

where the VI de baston shows two wild flowers

the VII de baston shows a tamed pole

where the VIII de baston shows two wild flowers

the VIIII de baston shows a tamed pole

the lion's colors are repeated in the skeleton

are repeated in the chevalier de baston

la maison diev's drops are repeated in the ace de bastons

are repeated in the ace de épée

the blaze (la maison diev) is repeated in the mandorla (le monde)

la pance's book is repeated in le batelevr's table

rhyme

the yellow sprout in the ace of baston rhymes with the fire in la maison diev

the fire in la maison diev rhymes with the water stream in temperance

temperance's vases rhyme with le toille's vases

le toille's black bird rhymes with lemperevur's black eagle

lemperevr's crossed legs rhyme with le pandv's crossed legs

le pandv's yellow hair rhymes with the sun rays in la maison diev

the building in la maison diev rhymes with the green branch in the ace of baston

the crawfish in la lvne rhymes with the flower in the IIII de épée

the scimitars in the IIII de épée rhyme with the mandorla in le monde

the mandorla in le monde rhymes with the chains in le diable

the chained couple in le diable rhymes with the II de covpe

the two fish in the II de covpe rhyme with the two dogs in la lvne

simile

the II de deniers looks like temperance's nipples

the II de deniers looks like a person looking at herself in the mirror

the II de deniers looks like two people signing a contract

the II de deniers looks like an old printing press printing a banner

the II de deniers looks like a D.J.'s turn-table

(ace de baston + v de covpe) all these women waiting for that bouquet like piranhas

(le monde + valet de baston) like coming home from work to find your son jerking off

(III de covpe + X de épée) like the winner at a knitting contest

Three Arguments (2+1) On The Concrete Poetics Of The Marseille Tarot (Where One Is Advised To Look At The Finger And Not At The Moon)

I

Words are affordable actions

I say Tom ate O you say

Are affordable anybody can have

Tomato a vowel sounds

The word 'elephant' anybody can go

All the other sounds a bird won't stay

Where Le Fol is going even the word 'ivory' is cheap

If all the others fly

II

I say "keep them on key"

you hear "keep the monkey"

I say "gobbling kingpin head"

you hear "gob blinking pinhead"

I say "at them all"

you hear "at the mall"

III

Le Tarot contient

(qu'on tient)

de 22 lames

(devin de lames)

ses leçons

(c'est le son)*

* the tarot contains it's lessons in 22 cards/the tarot cards the diviner holds are made of sound.

A LITTLE SAMPLER OF TAROLOGICAL DEVICES (II)

analogy

even the smallest pill can make you cough (*VIII de épée* + *VII de épée*)

she spent the whole night serving them (*VI de covpes* + *reine de covpes*)

onomatopoeia

vroom! (*la maison diev*)

thud… (*valet de baston*)

poof! (*le batalevr*)

drip, drip, drip *(le toille)*

ka-ching (*ace de deniers*)

whoosh! (*XIII*)

personification

they carried him in their arms (*X de covpe*)

she was dancing alone in the house (*IIII de épée*)

they were chatting when that bitch came in (*III de covpe*)

at first, she didn't know who to trust (*X de deniers*)

they were playing hide and seek in a corn field (*VIII de deniers*)

all that crisscrossing made them grow apart (*IIII de baston*)

they carried the coffin silently (*IIII de deniers*)

more rhymes

the crown in the ace de *épée* rhymes with the top of the ace *de covpe*

rhymes with la pances's crown rhymes with *la maison diev*'s crown

le diable's tongue rhymes with *le pandv*'s tongue

rhymes with la *maison diev*'s fire

the lion in *force* rhymes with the lion in *le monde*

rhymes with the creature in *le fol*

rhymes with the four *chevalier*'s horses

the two towers in *la lvne* rhyme with the two poles in *le pandv*

the cloud in the *ace de bastons* rhymes with the cloud in the *ace de épée*

rhymes with the cloud in *le ivgement*

the branch in the *ace de bastons* rhymes with the trumpet in *le ivgement*

rhyme scheme

the whole suit *de épée* rhymes with *le diable*

rhymes with *le monde*

the whole suit *de covpe* rhymes with the lion's mouth (*force*)

rhymes with the top of the building (*la maison diev*)

rhymes with the trumpet's mouth (*le ivgement*)

rhymes with *le fol*'s pouch

lemperevr and *imperatris* rhyme with *le pape* and la *pances* rhyme with the acolytes in *le pape* rhyme with the women in *lamovrev*

rhyme with the horses in *le charior* rhyme with the scales in *ivstice*

rhyme with the poles in *le pandv* rhyme with the vases in *temperance*

rhyme with the couple in *le diable* rhyme with the people in *la maison diev*

rhyme with the jars in *le toille* rhyme with the dogs in *la lvne*

rhyme with the twins in *le soleil* rhyme with the couple in *le ivgement*

rhyme with de *II de covpes* rhyme with de *II de deniers*

rhyme with de *II de baston* rhyme with de *II de épée*

rhyme with the two flowers in the *II, IIII, VI and VIII de baston*

rhyme with the blue swords in the *X de épée*

rhyme with the two heads in *XIII*

le pape rhymes with *le diable* rhymes with *le soleil*

rhymes with *la lvne* rhymes with the man in *le chariot*

rhymes with the man in *lamovrev* rhymes with *le pandv*

rhymes with the red swords and the flowers in the suit *deépée*

rhymes with the building in *la maison diev*

An Argument About Why Le Pandv Is The Only Card That Can Be Reversed

pips (180°)

a/e, b /q, d/p, e/a, m/w, n /u, o/o, p/d, q/b, s/s, u/n, w /m, x/x, z/z

trumps (180°)

H/H, I/I, M/W, N/N, O/O, S/S, W/M, X/X, Z/Z

trumps (90° clock-wise)

E/M, N/Z, U/C, W/E, Z/N, O/O, X/X

trumps (90° anti clock-wise)

C/U, E/W, M/E, N/Z, O/O, X/X, Z/N

the above argument makes evident how:

when some trumps and pips are reversed, they return to themselves

when most trumps and pips are reversed, they simply end up upside-down

only one of them truly become a new image when reversed

A Brief Antinumerological Manual

1.

a.

anoint an allegorical – neonatal, ironical, biennial, bicentennial, monomaniacal – number:

1969

b.

reincarnate it from an ungrammatical figure into an arguable one:

NINETEEN SIXTY NINE

c.

ruminate, reorient, or recombine it to unroll an oracular retelling:

INSENTIENT
INTESTINE
NINETEENS
INTENSITY
NINETEEN
SENTIENT
TINNIEST
ENTITIES
NINETIES
TEENIEST
ENTENTES
EXISTENT
ENTENTE
TINIEST
INTENTS
EXTENTS
INTENSE

NINNIES
TENSITY
SIXTEEN
TEENSY
SEXTET
ENTITY
EXTENT
TENNIS
INTENT
SETTEE
NINETY
TENETS
NINNY
SEINE
INSET
YETIS
NIXES
TEXTS
TINTS
TINNY
NEXTS
TENET
NINES
TEENY
EXITS
NITES

TEENS
TENTS
NISEI
EXIST
TENSE
TESTY
STINT
SIXTY
STEIN
TINES
STET
TEST
TEEN
SITE
EXIT
TEES
TINY
SEXY
NEST
NEXT
TINS
TENT
YINS
SENT
TENS
SEEN

NETT
TEXT
SINE
NITS
TINT
NITE
NETS
SNIT
TINE
TIES
STYE
EYES
INNS
YENS
TITS
YETI
EXES
NINE
SEE
INS
NET
STY
NIT
ITS
TIN
TEE

YIN
SEX
TIT
YET
YES
INN
YEN
NEE
XIS
SIN
SIT
TIE
TIS
EYE
SET
SIX
TEN
ENS
NIX
IN
YE
EX
IT
IS
EN
TI

XI

1

d.

to recite a cool nonnumerological omen, reinforce a congruent murmur:

INN
SENTIENT EYES
SIN NEXT
EXIT: SEXY
TEEN'S
TINY NEST

2.

BIRDS made of NUMBERS, NUMBERS

made of WORDS, WORDS

made of BIRDS

3.

NUMBERS = NUM BIRDS

Colormeaning (Moronic Angel)

1.

colors are words
with limited anagrammatic properties.

example:

red = re, ed

blue = lube, be

yellow = lowly, yowl, well, yell, low, ole, woe, yew, lye, owl, owe, yow, ell, we, ow, yo, lo, ye

green = genre, gene, nee, erg, gee, ere, re, en

orange = groan, argon, range, goner, anger, organ, gear, rage, aeon, gore, earn, rang, gone, ogre, roan, ergo, goer, near, nor, nae, roe, ear, nag, ran, ore, ago, rag, gar, one, erg, era, eon, age, ego, oar, are, or, en, on, an, go, re, no, a

purple = upper, pulp, lure, pure, pule, rule, purl, prep, rep, per, pep, pup, rue, re, up

black = balk, back, lack, calk, cab, alb, lac, lab, la, a

white = withe, wite, thew, with, whit, whet, wit, the, tie, hie, wet, hit, hew, it, we, ti, hi, eh, he, I

2.

these anagrammatic properties can be expanded by combining two or more colors

example:

red + green = reneged, greened, greener, render, renege, degree, gender, erred, greed, green, edger, genre, deer, need, reed, gene, rend, geed, nerd, edge, err, erg, ere, end, red, gee, nee, den, ed, en, re

3.

the whole spectrum of language can be reached by the successive combination of all known colors, or vice versa

4.

in any sentence, a color scheme can be detected

example:

an ogre with lube on his back hit a cab with a yowl = orange + white + blue + black + white + black + white + yellow

this is:

an ogre (orange) with (white) lube (blue) on his back (black) hit (white) a cab (black) with (white) a yowl (yellow)

4.

in any color scheme, a sentence can be detected

example:

green + purple + green + white = genre: pure gene wite

6.

by extension, any synonym for any of the words contained in a color's name would stand for that very color

example:

an ogre (orange) = a giant (orange) = a troll (orange)
a cab (black) = a taxi (black)

7.

any time we read a sentence we are inadvertently seeing colors

any time see a color we are inadvertently reading words

NOTE: this color scheme is guaranteed to be as useless as any other symbolic system.

KEYS

A Chapter Where The Marseille Tarot's Key Is Given, While Hinting At The Fact That The Meaning Of An Image Is The Sound We Make When We Describe It, All Done With Such Simplicity That The Formula Itself Is Shorter Than Its Title

there is no[1]thing to[2] it

there is no[3]thing to[4] eat

there is no[5]thing, tweet

[1] this letter 'o' is the 139th letter in Jackes Prévert's poem "Pour faire le portrait d'un oiseaux"

[2] this letter 'o' is the 51st letter in Raymond Rousell's "Nouvelles Impressions d'Afrique", Canto II: "Le champ the bataill des pyramides"

[3] this letter 'o' is the 302th letter in bp Nichol's "Probable Systems 14: Re-discovery of the 22 letter alphabet: an archaeological report"

[4] this letter 'o' is the third to last letter in Victor Hugo's "A Hieroglyphic Alphabet" (translated by Steve McCaffery)

[5] this letter 'o' is the 6th letter on the 6th line in Victor Coleman's "queen" poem. Somehow this letter o bears an extraordinary resemblance with the 16th letter in Aleksei Kruchenykh's poem "Heights", but we are not sure about the actual procedence of Mr. Coleman's vowels.

SPECIAL OFFER: every tarot reading now comes with a complementary plastic fly. (Find something that stinks, place the fly on top of it and walk away.)

A Color Is Fossil Light (after A peRson Whom all rEad)

*(now)*some colors are more colorful than others*(you will)* some others are a colorful tan*(realize the reason)*white is not the best white*(why La Papesse's)*the best white is black*(book is colored)*black is not the best black*(as flesh)*the best black is red*(while her face)*red is not the best red*(remains white)*the best red is blue*(the book)*blue is not the best blue*(is the woman's)*the best blue is yellow*(forehead)*yellow is not the best yellow*(where*

all)the best yellow is green***(her frowning)***green is not the best green***(has been)***the best green is white***(written down)***

(All) Images Outlined (With Similar) Shapes Share (The Same) Qualities (And All Refer To The Same) Thing*

ha ha! · sense into nonsense · **ah ha!** · nonsense in to sense · **ha ha!** · sensing tune on sense · **ah ha!** · them arse say "tarot" · **ha ha!** · non sensing to sense · **ah ha!** · zen zing to non zen · **ha ha!** · non zen zing to zen · **ah ha!**

* All the words between parenthesis belong to Jean-Pierre Brisset. The rest of the words came from ebay.

Every Word Was Ounce a Poem / Every Word Was Once a Pound

Fools and Reapers* contain a language that follows a syntax of backbones and limbs. Look at them long enough and you will see them open up into a series of doubles and matchings, into a terrain of fidgets and twitches each one containing the other.

* 'abcdefghijklmnopqrstuvwxyz' is a name · a skeleton is an alphabet · a bone is a consonant · our bowels uttering our vowels · every breath is a quotation · our body against our vowels · this is quoting · our bowels push our teeth · the-en-A is the poem · you an anagram of me · hand is anagram for ribcage · ribcage is anagram for fish · fish is anagram for foot · foot is anagram for twenty-two · 22 are the bones · we mime a sign to mine its meaning · our vowels are our bowels · a consonant is bone · naming is anagramming · bones of an alphabet · a skeleton is 'abcdefghijklmnopqrstuvwxyz'

NOTE: the 4th, 5th, 6th, 7th, 8th, 9th, 10th, 11th, 15th, 16th, 18th, 19th, 20th, 21st, 22nd, 23rd, 25th, 26th, 27th, 28th, 29th, 30th, 34th, 35th, 36th, 37th, 41st, and 43rd words in this text belong to Robert Smithson. The rest of the words in this text are in the public domain.

How Come We Don't Use Birds Instead Of Spoons To Stir Our Coffee? (Seven Instances Where a Tarot Card Was Deployed In a Non-Divination Context)

1.

a woman is looking for a man.

I tell her I know the perfect candidate. I proceed to describe a gentleman to her. I describe the gentleman's features in detail. When I am done, I reach into my pocket and take *Lemperevr*. I tell her that's the man. I give the card to the woman. I instruct her to carry the image in her purse, to compare any gentleman she may meet with the man depicted in the card until she finds a match.

2.

a woman takes the subway escalator carrying a book on the *danse macabre*. I follow her down the escalator. I reach into my pocket and take *La Morte*. The cover of her book depicts a Grim Reaper. *La Morte* depicts a Grim Reaper. I touch the woman's shoulder and offer her the card while saying "I think you dropped this". The woman takes *La Morte*.

when the subway arrives, the woman and I take separate cars.

3.

a man sits in a cafe and writes on his computer. I peek over his shoulder. He is writing a story titled "the fortuneteller". I interrupt him. I give him a card: *La Maison Diev*. I tell him it's for "inspiration". He seems bothered by it. I wonder if he will finish that story.

4.

a bald man in a coffee shop asks me if I am a jewelry designer. I tell him I am a fortuneteller. He asks me if I have a tarot card with me. I say "yes". I give him *Le Fov*. He takes a picture of the card with his IPhone and records some mumblings in it. He fidgets with an app. After two minutes, he shows me *Le Fov* on the iPhone's screen: *Le Fov* is walking and mumbling. The man tells me: "that's what I do". Then he walks out the door.

5.

I hear about a tailor who collects taxidermy. I take *Le Diable*, write "to be read in private" on its back and mail it to the tailor.

I haven't heard back from him.

6.

in a bookshop, the man behind the counter mentions it's his birthday. I give him a card: *Le Soleil*. The man points to the window and shows me that it is raining. He says he was just hoping for some sun.

I told him that's what birthdays are for.

7.

inside POETRY MAGAZINE I find a self-addressed envelop intended for subscriptions. I put the *Ace de Deniers* in the envelop and mail it to the magazine.

I haven't gotten my first issue yet.

DISCLAIMER: what is poetic about the marseille tarot is not its subject matter or its alleged purpose, but the way in which we look at it · using the tarot to interfere with the everyday is a way to interfere with the tarot's social function · let's substitute the 'I' for the 'eye' · the eyes leave no trace of their wonderings, but the mouth betrays them · when we look at

the tarot we don't peek, we don't stare, we perform: we take form-per-form apart and we put form-per-form back together, so the tarot's mythology won't eat its metaphors · the poetics of the marseille tarot are not concerned with the making of poems, but with the poetry of making · what matters is the tarot's matter, its material form, not what it "means" but what it is · any poetic form is a provisional thought that informs us (it hold us up within the logic of its forms) · the marseille tarot's images are there to be experienced · not all experiences can be put into words · our response to tarot doesn't need to be 'understanding' (standing-under our reasonable assumptions) · our response to a card could be a gasp, a question, an apple, or another card · our response to an image doesn't have to be coherent, nor even transmissible to others in some unequivocal way · puzzlement (puzzle t men) is expansive · the tarot is frozen, melt it with your breath

XIII, An Aim Without A Name

XIII, an aim without a name, is coming back inside the picture**AS IF WE COULD BE WOKEN TO WORDS WHILE ASLEEP TO LANGUAGE***look! its head is still out of it**AS IF WE CAN ENVISION THE BRAIN**this little detail should suffice as evidence of the fact that the skeleton depicted in XIII, an aim without a name, can get in and out of the card at will**INHABITING THE DARKEST VAULT**this detail should also provide ample proof of the fact that the skeleton came out of the card's frame to erase its name with its scythe**AS IF WE CAN SEE SYNAPSES**even so, we must firmly decline any inclination to suspect that the absence of words would result in silence**AS SPARKS OF LIGHT**silence is harvested language**AS IF WE WOULD SEE STARS**XIII, an aim without a name, erased its name, so its name can be heard

 * while the words: "as", "asleep", "be", "could", "if", "language", "to", "we", while", "woken", and "words" are in the public domain, the phrase "as if we could be woken to words while asleep to language" belongs to Mr. Charles Bernstein

 THIS MESSAGE IS BROUGHT TO YOU by Alfred Jarry's letter 'r' · we cloned that additional letter 'r' Alfred Jarry slipped in the first word of his play Ubu Roi · now you can have that letter 'r' too · slip an 'r' in any word of your choice! amaze your friends! in your mouth, a "thought" will become a "trhougth" and "white" will be "wrhite" · swerve away and swerve a way through the monotonous verbosity of your daily life! for a limited time only

A Chapter Where The Tarot Is Defined As A 'System Of Deviations', And Also As Something Else

preface

we don't need

the possibility

to read

of meaning

the tarot as much

is more

as to think

meaningful than

about the idea of

meaning itself

the tarot

1.

TAROT = image + time

margins are the most powerful part of a tarot card

it is at the margins that time enters the picture

any image exists in a qualitative time-frame where everything is happening at the same time

and everything continues happening without regard of the actual pass of chronological time

if we align two or more cards in a sequence, we introduce the notion of 'before' and 'after'

those white margins account for the chronological distance

between the events depicted on the first card and the events depicted on the second card

2.

TAROT = a stone for striking matches

this definition is self-evident

we won't insult the reader's intelligence by explaining it

3.

TAROT = a system of deviations

each trump is the clinamen of the previous one

and the whole tarot becomes our own clinamen

(clean a men clay naming a clean amen)

either by waking us up and having us swerving away from a dream

or by keeping us dreaming, and having us swerving away from being awake

the tarot's effectivity can be measured by how fast it would take us to where we weren't going

4.

TAROT = the darkness at the beginning of the tunnel

the tarot is very wise

except when

the tarot is very stupid

epilogue

the fact of tarot

is very different

from the act of tarot

TAROT TROUVÉ

The world has no quarrel

with the tarot images

but with what it is said about them

Don't change the images

change the words

TAROT TROUVÉ

To be re-found

the tarot had to be found

Thanks Jean-Claude Flornoy

Thanks my friend

in memory of Jean-Claude Flornoy (Paris 1950 – Sainte-Suzanne 2011),

who taught me that you don't make images, but images make you.

The Tarot S Peek But Eye Cannot Here
(first tarot-poetics workshop's admission form)

Wordplay seems to be a most appropriate tool for interrogating the Marseill tarot. Not only are the words in the cards full of puns *(le bateleur, la maison dieu, lemonde)*, but it is through punning that the Marseille tarot's folklore urges us to inquire about the true nature of these images: *"Le Tarot contient de 22 lames ses leçons/Le Tarot qu'on tient, devin de lames, c'est le son"*. Wordplay is also what links the Marseille tarot to that lineage of poets who saw punning as a detour toward some kind of unexpected "truth" (Roussel, Jarry, Brisset, Leiris, Breton, Peréc...). When it comes to interrogating the Marseille tarot, poetry should be more fruitful than prose. Our workshop aims to create a space for such inquiry. Applicants should respond *to* this application form.

Practical Assignments

PART 1.

1.

nail an I

on god to

get gold

2.

to make snow poke

a sugar pack

3.

yawn until the O yawns back

PART 2. *LA RÉAPPARITION* (after Georges Perec *La Disparition*)

the addition of an **E** at the end of a word will make it sweeter:

sweet*e*

violent*e*

hemorrhoid*e*

take all the letters **E** Georges Perec didn't use in his novel *La Disparition*

for a week, place one of these letters **E** at the end of each single word you say

QUESTION THE FOLLOWING ANSWERS:

1.

whomever spells

a word owns

whomever listens

2.

a vowel blows the body up

making the utter able

3.

when you see the eyes go on

when you seek the eyes bounce back

4.

LIFE is written wrong

it should be **ILFE**

5.

a lake is a big, BIG, leak

6.

a fish looks like an eye

an eye looks like a bug

a bug looks like a sun

a sun looks like an eye

an eye looks

7.

a queue is an **O** that grew a tail: **Q**

8.

The **C** can **K** but the **K** can't **C**

CONSIDER THE POSITION OF *L'ARCANE SANS NOM*:

M is the 13th letter counting forward

N is the 13th letter counting backward

M and N stand at the center of the alphabet

M an(-d) N = MAN

('d' is the first letter of that name that can't be named)

WRITTE AN ESSAY:

Please, quote a pigeon

This form should be emailed to a complete stranger. Proven that the stranger is strange enough, emailing the form will guarantee your automatic admission in this workshop. The workshop will take place in an undisclosed location. Be sure not to lett us where that is.

WARNING: having a ballon as your first toy can turn wooden blocks into lethal weapons.

Word Fisher: Whirred Fissure

We have been immersed in language for most of our lives.

Language is part of our landscape, and as such, it has become invisible.

We don't look at words, we "know" what they mean.

Imagine that, one day, your are riding the subway absent-mindedly staring at a poster,

staring at a word, a word like 'stop'.

You have seen that word before.

You have seen that word so many times that you don't see it anymore.

That day you notice that if you turn it around it becomes the word 'dots'.

As you step in the word you step out of the world, out of the way you use language.

There is a pleasant sense of unavoidability in finding 'dots' inside of 'stop'.

As you draw a line between these two words, a light goes on in your head.

The word 'dots' makes you see the word 'stop' in a very precise way.

Each word informs and affects what you think about the other one.

More important, the whole happenstance opens your words to many other worlds.

You start looking around and 'around' becomes 'a round' while 'looking' becomes 'Lou King' and 'you start' a 'juice tart'.

The poetry of the Word, the way each word takes you to another

unexpected word in a way that feels both capricious and unavoidable, reveals itself to you.

The tarot is another language,

another landscape we have made invisible out of our own familiarity with it.

We don't look at the cards, we "know" what they mean.

One day you find the stream of water Temperance is juggling hiding in the flames of The Tower.

You look at The Hermit and notice that his lantern looks like the Ace of Cups.

The Hermit makes you see the Ace of Cups in a very precise way.

Temperance reveals ideas about The Tower that the Tower couldn't show you on its own.

Each card informs and affects the way you think about the other card.

As you draw lines between these cards many lights go on in your head.

The poetry of the Marseille tarot, the way each card takes you to another unexpected card in a way that feels both capricious and unavoidable,

reveals itself to you.

The Tarot Doesn't Care About You (How To Let The Tarot Rule You Life)

"The tarot is a critique of the mechanization of reason"

Paul Nagy

"I can't imagine a spiritual way of life that isn't impersonal, dependent on chance, never on efforts of the will."

Georges Bataille

PREMISE:

Tarot is the soul of slapstick.

As a score for the performance of daily life the tarot turns the soothing effects of saying into the liberating joy of an indifferent execution.

By becoming an operation manual for life the tarot turns the telling effects of fortune into an eloquent state of detached enactment in which the actor (this is YOU) relinquishes all control over the present moment and blindly follows the tarot images.

The actor is given a performative space within his/her own body

and endowed with a disregard of the purpose behind each one of his/her actions.

As long as the actor regards him/herself **AS AN ACTOR** he/she will be free.

THE CONTRACT:

The actor agrees to carry the tarot pack on him/her at all times. The actor will give up the desire to control what he/she is doing. The actor agrees to let the tarot define every single action he/she takes. The actor will clear up his/her mind of any action that has not been suggested by the tarot. The actor agrees to defer any decision-making to the random draw of a card. The actor will let his/her actions be actions rather than expressions of his own will.

The tarologist agrees to be on call 24/7, ready to provide technical support to the actor. The tarologist will give up the desire to control or affect the actor's actions. The tarologist will clear up his mind of any opinion about the actions suggested by the tarot. The tarologist will let the actor's actions become an expression of the tarot's (lack of) will rather than projections of his own ego.

INSTALLATION:

(Upon signing of THE contract)

The tarologist will give the actor a pack of cards (trumps only).

The tarologist will instruct the actor to leave the tarot pack on top of his/her bedside table before going to sleep.

The tarologist will give the actor the following instructions:

INSTRUCTIONS:

As soon as you wake up, take the trumps and shuffle them.

Pull one card from the tarot pack.

Do whatever the character in the card is doing. Do it as LITERALLY as possible.

For example: If you pull The Wheel of Fortune, you should keep tossing and turning over your mattress all day long. If you pull La Papesse, you should grab a book and spend the morning reading in bed. If you pull The Sun, you should go and stare at yourself in the bathroom mirror wearing only your underwear. If you pull The Fool, you should leave on foot. If you pull The Tower, you should jump out the window.

Whenever you feel the need to change the activity, pull another card.

IMPORTANT: You can only pull a new card AFTER the action suggested by the previous card has been enacted.

TROUBLESHOOTING:

By following the tarot blindly the actor walks the line between intention and misunderstanding. If the actor doesn't know how to apply the tarot's instructions to a given situation, the tarologist will help. In case of any doubt regarding the action suggested by any specific trump the actor can call the tarologist for technical support. The extent of such support will be limited by the terms of the TROUBLESHOOTING PACKAGE purchased by the actor at the moment of the installation. The TROUBLESHOOTING PACKAGE substitutes the tarologist's fee.

VERY EXPENSIVE PACKAGE

Upon calling the tarologist, the purchasers of the Very Expensive Package will be told exactly what to do. No need for the actor to assume any kind of personal responsibility in the happenstances of his/her own life. We got it all covered*.

EXPENSIVE PACKAGE

Upon calling the tarologist, the purchasers of the Expensive Package will be provided with two or more possible interpretations of the actions depicted in a card. These actions would then be tailored to fit the situation at hand. Technically, the choice of interpretation will be left to the actor, but the tarologist may hint at the right one by the inflections in his voice.

CHEAP PACKAGE

The Cheap Package only entitles the actor to listen to a pre-recorded answer from the tarologist saying: *"The card you got is the card you got. Deal with it!"*

VERY CHEAP PACKAGE

Upon calling the tarologist, the purchasers of the Very Cheap Package will always receive the same instructions: *"The answer is inside of you. Your higher self is your better half. Listen to your inner voice!"*

Sign up now! Let your indifference make the difference!

WARNING: as tempting as it may be to use the tarot as a score performance for the rest of your life,

it would be better if you only do it for limited periods of time ranging between 1 and 24 hours.

* Actually, nothing is covered. Neither our Very Expensive Package nor any of the other packages includes insurance of any kind. Although the tarologist will claim any personal success the actor may have as a direct consequence of his insights (it is good for business), any personal hazard or embarrassment occurred as a result of letting the tarot dictate the actor's actions, as well as any damage to third parties that may result from this practice, will be the actor's sole responsibility.

Com(parable) Language

ATTENTION: if you ever had a reading with me, please disregard whatever I told you and assume I meant the exact opposite. I just found out that I got the whole thing backwards. (Sorry, no refunds, only re-found).

1. Just as a new sound makes an old sound fade, or like a new sight takes our mind away from the previous one, a tarot card always trumps the one preceding it.

2. Since the last card rules the sequence, a tarot sentence should be read from right to left: object – verb – subject.

3. In a sequence, the third card is always affecting the first card by deploying the actions depicted in the second card.

4. The second card takes on the functions of a verb: Le Chariot would then become "to chariot", La Maison Diev would become "to tower", Le Soleil would be "to sun", or La Lune would be "to moon".

5. These verbs can be deployed through their semantic value ("To fool" would mean to deceive a person to our own advantage); through their phonetic value ("to sun": too soon), or through their visual value ("to chariot" is to trample over a landscape in order to get what we want. "To emperor" is to sit back and hold our ground, or our pants).

6. Some trumps offer more than one of these possibilities. ("to tower" could be to impose ourselves over someone smaller;

but it could also mean throwing someone out of the window, to fall, or to collapse. "To fool" can be to pull a con or to walk away from a wild dog).

7. The context of the sentence would define in which way we deploy these verbs. (Next to Le Pandv, La Morte would mean "to cut down", but next to Le Soleil it would mean "to erase", next to Lestoille it would mean "to harvest" and next to Lemperatrise it would mean "to kill").

8. A tarot sentence* is not a message. To say that La Papesse "moons" the Lover is to state a fact. Taken to signify "to put some distance between two towers by means of a body of water, a crayfish and two dogs", the verb "to moon" simply makes evident how the cards describe a woman pulling away from a rather lubricated situation.

9. The tarot's semantics should be as capricious, idiosyncratic, and ruled by exceptions as the semantics of any other language.

NOTE: the method outlined above would benefit from some examples. Figure them out yourself.

* The Marseille tarot speaks to the eye. Deaf eyes need words. A tarot sentence is not the tarot. The tarot can't be interpreted, only experienced.

Coda

By stating that the letter R resembles a head in profile, with a big round nose and a stick-out beard, we hope to elicit an analogical thought-process that will have the reader finding the likeness of such letter in Lemperevr, or in Cyrano de Bergerac. We do so while hoping that the same analogical process would have the reader seeing the VII de épée as a chicken's bone stuck in a dog's throat, or as the sound of a needle falling on a marble floor.

By stating that the setter R contains the letter P, and also the I, or the K, and somehow the B; or by stating that the letter O contains the letter G and the letter Q; just as the letter D contains both the letters I and O, we hope to evidence how the typographic consistencies among letters, where the details in each letter resonate with the rest of the alphabet by a sense of visual coherence, is in itself a poetic pattern*. (Poetry might be that realm where the alphabet is not compelled to behave like language). These very same poetic patterns, which manifest in the consonance of the details among cards, are the ones we find in the Marseille tarot; so one could say that both the Marseille tarot and the alphabet are poems whose rhythm tickles the eye before any sound is made, or any sense is given to their forms**.

*A rhymes with K rhymes with M rhymes with N rhymes with V rhymes with W rhymes with X rhymes with Y rhymes with Z

E rhymes with B rhymes with F rhymes with L rhymes with T (F rhymes with P rhymes with R)

I rhymes with **E** rhymes with **F** rhymes with **K** rhymes with **L** rhymes with **N**

O rhymes with **C** rhymes with **D** rhymes with **G** rhymes with **Q** rhymes with **S**

U rhymes with **J**

**If we recur to such antics is because we believe the alphabet to be a very apt model to explain the Marseille tarot's visual language. Both are systems conformed by a limited set of elements whose original meaning has been lost. This loss allows us to generate new meanings by permuting the elements of both systems in more or less infinite ways.

Sometimes, a sequence of such elements would say something:

PLASTIC

Which in turn would hide something else:

P(LAST)IC

Sometimes what it is said would recall the sound of other things:

plasSTIC

Sometimes a simple twist can transform what is being said:

P

LASTIC

E

Sometimes, the same elements can be visually grouped in more than one way:

WOMEN SCREAM

WOMENS CREAM

Or they can be physically rearranged so the same elements form a completely different picture:

HARD, FEASABLE

READABLE FISH

ARS TAROTICA

1. The tarot's trumps are divided as follow:

21 minor arcana
5 major arcana

2. We can find meaning in their original order.
Example:

abcdefghijklmnopqrstuvwxyz
  b   ij   o   u x

3. Rearranged, the same few trumps can say quite different things.
Example:

Picasso ogling
panics gigolos
so pig, solacing,
pissing coal
go-go social pings slop
casino gig, slicing goops
a cola going sips

4. A tarot trump can mean more than one thing.
Example:

cops wear wife beaters down

5. It is just a matter of giving things a second glance.
Example:

the tarologist spun
the tarologist's pun

6. A tarot trump always contains a bit of the other trumps.
Example:

women
 omen
 o men
 o n

7. Those bits and pieces are messages.
Example:

millennium
 ill
m en

8. Sometimes these messages seem logical.
Example:

obscene
 scene

morning
 r ing

9. But the good ones leave us puzzled.
Example:

facsimile
 s mile

because it is necessary
be s   c   ary

mirror image
m or   e
 r   age

10. The game consists of seeing beyond what seems obvious
Example:

SLEIGHT

About the author

enrique enriquez \'vizh-wəl-'thiŋkər\

noun. Usage: often attributive

1: any of the various mammals that are usually solitary or sometimes live in pairs and have the young open-eyed and furred at birth
2: a person whose job is to prevent or put an end to leaks of sensitive information

Enrique Enriquez (Caracas, 1969) is a tarot reader. His work with the Marseille Tarot hasn't granted him any award, monetary compensation nor any other form of prestige whatsoever. He is not affiliated with any respectable institutions. He doesn't know important people nor can he be associated with any celebrity. Thanks of this persistent state of dereliction he has been able to develop a deep understanding of the tarot's poetics, without having to endure the distractions of fame and derailments of success. He lives in New York with his wife and his three kids.

CPSIA information can be obtained at www.ICGtesting.com
Printed in the USA
LVOW132130230412

278762LV00002B/9/P

9 788792 633125